7 KEY PRINCIPLES
OF
QUALITY CARE

By

Bert Nemcik, Ph.D.

Lifelong Learning Network

Copyright © 2015

TABLE OF CONTENTS

DEDICATION

To Mom and Dad: two important people in my life who taught me to pursue learning with wonder and amazement, and to see every challenge as a way to learn something new.

MOTTO

"You don't have a problem, IF you have a solution."
Bert Nemcik

Every program can benefit by adopting principles that guide its employees in their delivery of services. I hope that those who read this book are inspired to doing quality work with the people you serve. As the motto above says, solutions eliminate the need for us to dwell on the problem. This book is one of the solutions to an age-old problem for programs that struggle with keeping quality care as the focus.

INTRODUCTION

If you work with people, this book was written for you. The principles contained within are applicable in any human service milieu. Quality care is everyone's business not just the quality improvement person.

What is quality care? It is the application of the mission and principles that motivate and inspire all of us to provide the best care possible to the people we serve.

How can it be that simple?
It can if we just live by and support sound principles that promote quality. How we systematically provide the best care possible is the subject of this text.

Let me explain.

There are many people who choose to work as counselors, social workers, case workers, probation officers, psychologists, therapists and teachers who have the best intentions in mind when they begin their careers. They are driven by a genuine desire to make the world a better place to live. For a time they are successful at guiding and supporting humans who are in need of their assistance. Eventually they run out of steam, motivation, will power and the desire to serve others. The systems they work in are not set up to insure their ultimate success. They butt heads with administration, face budget cuts that restrict services, and eventually leave the profession expressing the notion they are "burned out."

What causes this to happen to so many people who enter the profession with the highest ideals? It's not that people are weak and not prepared. It's not the program's administration that is trying to balance quality service with the spreadsheet. It's a lack of guiding principles that all can live by regardless of the system in which they work.

Edwards Demming, the father of the Japanese business renaissance, maintained that the principles a system promotes are responsible for 85% of the success or failure of an enterprise. He pioneered systems thinking by stating the idea that when a system is failing, don't blame the people. Look at the system and evaluate its principles. He presented elaborate ways to fix systems. American businesses discounted his ideas, so he went to Japan and was readily embraced by Japanese business. The rest is history.

If you think about what he believed, his ideas make a lot of sense. If people work within a system that is not guided by solid principles, then the chances of their being successful are greatly reduced. On the other hand, if people work in a system that is founded on solid principles, they are much more likely to succeed. Demming demonstrated this by changing an entire culture that was ravaged from war. He applied his principles in a systematic way and revamped the entire Japanese economy. It remains today, second only to the United States, as a world economic power.

Principles are the guiding forces that bind civilizations together. The oldest set is now more than 6000 years old and was first recorded on two stone tablets. I'm referring to the Ten Commandments. First, the Hebrews lived by them. The early Christians, who were mainly Jewish, continued to live by them after Christ died. The history of the last two millennia is the record of societies that tried to abide by them and either succeeded or failed. They are principles that challenge people to live by a moral code that has faced the test of time. They are the core belief of the Christian world.

Now, we could just adopt them as the foundation of our work, but there would be some people who are not Christians who would balk at the thought. Religious overtones would affect people of different faiths. This does not mean that these 10 simple commandments have no place in the human service profession.

On the contrary, they are always operative even if they aren't visibly displayed on the walls of the agency, or in the homes of the people being served.

The point is that there is an overwhelming need for principles that are clear and easy to follow so that people can provide the best care possible. In order to provide a structure to this system we call human services, we need to find principles that will guide and support everyone's efforts, remove the fear of failure, and motivate us to consistently strive to provide the highest quality service to people.

With this goal in mind, The 7 Key Principles of Quality Care are being shared with you. I believe you will find them to be all-inclusive and applicable to any milieu in which you work. Most of all, they can be used to guide your own life, your family, the communities, schools and organizations to which you belong.

I hope you find reading this book as stimulating and inspiring as it has been for me to write.

Once you have finished, I encourage your comments on your learning experience. You can contact me the following ways:

EMAIL: bnemcik@yahoo.com

Forward!

Bert

7 KEY PRINCIPLES OF QUALITY CARE

<u>PEOPLE SECURITY</u> - Being with people and meaningfully interacting with them.

<u>PROGRAM INTEGRITY</u> - Providing a high degree of structure and clear expectations.

<u>ACCOUNTABILITY/ RESPONSIBILITY/ HIGH EXPECTATIONS</u> - Teaching responsibility by expecting people to accept accountability for their behavior.

<u>TEAM WORK and COMMUNICATION</u> - Working together and effectively communicating with one another.

<u>POSITIVE ROLE MODELING</u> - Teaching people by setting an example.

<u>DIGNITY AND RESPECT</u> - Showing care and concern for all people's needs.

<u>ENVIRONMENT OF CARE</u> – Maintaining a clean environment that promotes the physical and mental health of the people we serve.

PEOPLE SECURITY

"Being with people and meaningfully interacting with them"

People Security is being with people and meaningfully interacting with them. All human beings have the need for security. It is the second most basic need after physiological needs like food, clothing, water and shelter are met. Security has an all-encompassing quality about it. We feel secure when the people who love us spend time with us. If we don't have a sense of security early in our lives, we are apt to spend a significant part of our later years making sure that we are secure. This definition of security includes physical, mental, emotional and spiritual security. If we are to provide quality care to human beings, it is essential that we promote **People Security** in all of the services we provide. This need is first experienced in the prenatal condition and continues to be important the rest of life. Let me explain in more detail.

People are born. Upon entering the world beyond the womb, they are absolutely helpless. Unlike all other mammals, birds, invertebrates, mollusks and crustaceans, they must be protected and nurtured until they are almost adults. This places a significant burden on their parents. Just a few hours after a deer gives birth to a fawn, it is standing and nursing. Within a few months, it is ready to live on its own. Everywhere in the natural world, offspring are independent of their parents within months, and at most, a few years. The human being is unique because it doesn't reach maturity for more than a decade. Sometimes, it takes longer if there are extenuating circumstances that cause the child to require a prolonged maturation period.

According to Rousseau, they are "tabula Rasa," or blank sheets upon which parents, grandparents, communities, societies and civilizations imprint morals, values and beliefs.

Even though a child may develop physically in a normal way, there are times when this imprinting doesn't occur. The child doesn't approach adulthood with these in place. When moral development is retarded, refused, or denied, then the child often responds inappropriately to social conventions. If a child is reached early enough, the normal process of maturation may continue without too much fallout. If not, then there may be a need for more intense intervention in his or her life.

When the principle of **People Security** is employed, parents, grandparents, extended family members, teachers, guardians, Boy and Girl Scout leaders, pastors, Sunday school teachers, coaches and other interested adults become a viable part of a child's life. This insures that the child will develop and mature into a healthy, happy human being. When people security is not, the odds are reversed.

What is it that these people do that makes the difference? They are present in the child's life and meaningfully interacting with him.

Being present with a person means we are with them. This means we are actually where the person is and involved with him.

We've all heard of "quality time". This was one of those catchy phrases that described what absentee parents claimed they provided their children. Quality time meant that whatever time they spent with their children was "quality time". Since they didn't have a lot of time to spend, they believed they needed to intensify the interaction. It's hard to imagine that thirty minutes a day can substitute for being with a child and meaningfully interacting with him. How intense can a relationship if the relationship is bound by time?

The quality of a relationship isn't time bound. In fact, quality time is a contradiction. Any time spent with a child when some meaningful interaction is taking place is what I consider quality time.

It can involve something as simple as eating dinner together, something families do less and less as lifestyles grow more complex. It can be working together on a project like fixing something around the house or building a model. It can be cuddling up on a couch and watching TV. Yes, watching the TV can be meaningful interaction if the content has some morally redeeming value. Even if it doesn't, the time spent is meaningful because parent and child are together. I truly believe my son learned how to be a good catcher, not by my teaching him how to do it, but by lying next to me on the couch and watching great catchers like Johnny Bench work behind the plate. Yes, I answered his questions and pointed out what Bench was doing, but I think that just being together nurtured in my son a love of the game and a zest for catching.

Let's pursue this theme further. Imagine for a moment, an entire family watching "Forest Gump", "Gandhi" or "Gone with the Wind". The thematic content of the movies provides hours and hours of discussion matter. Long after the movie is over, fathers and sons, mothers and daughters can reflect back on what they watched and share ideas with one another. History, culture and moral issues are all presented in these entertaining and inspiring films. Again, I was surprised when my rough and tough son told me one day that "Gone with the Wind" was one of his favorite movies. He said that it made him think about how hard it must have been for people to have to decide what was right and wrong when it came to this issue of slavery. This is just one outcome of such a meaningful interaction.

Being with people is sometimes tough when the demands of modern living bear down upon us. We work, we try to exercise, and we go to the store and shop, drive home in rush hour traffic and arrive home worn out. Sometimes, the last thing adults want to do is spend time with others, let alone with demanding little children who have waited all day for Mommy and Daddy to come home.

Yet, if we don't do it, we shirk our responsibility to provide **People Security**. They want from us the sense that they are important, that spending time with them is the most significant part of our day. When they feel secure, they can approach living in a complex world with a greater sense of purpose and confidence. This is the goal of all parenting and it begins simply with our providing them with this sense of security as they develop into the kind of people who can leave home some day and be happy, healthy human beings.

Our profession is to provide quality services to children, adolescents or adults. Every job requires its paperwork, red tape and endless responsibilities that seem to get in the way of being with those we are treating. This is no excuse for not being with them. It is just a statement of reality.

When you consider that a client who is placed in a residential setting for any length of time spends fully a third of that time sleeping, is it any wonder that the time just seems to slip past? For example, in many residential programs, clients are in residence for an average of nine months. For three months, they are sleeping. Two months are spent going to school six hours a day. Another month is spent eating and walking back to the dorm. Another month is spent doing personal hygiene. Another month is scheduled for recreation, room time and moving from one place to another. When the final tally is made, about *three weeks* is spent in direct clinical services with the client. This doesn't mean that any of these other activities are not therapeutic. No, it is just a reminder that most time is not directly focused on what is considered to be clinical activity.

It is hard to swallow, but this is the reality of residential placement. It is critical then that we make every interaction a meaningful one. We can't be sitting in the office doing paperwork eight hours a day and hope that our clients will feel a sense of **People Security**.

Just being in the same building with them is not enough. They have to experience us. They have to hear and see and possibly touch us to know we are real. We aren't superhuman beings. We are professionals who have a profound impact on their lives when we provide this security for them. It's not a magical process. Sometimes it takes time and effort to just get up from the desk and walk to where the clients are and spend some time with them.

Given the figures presented in the last paragraph, you can see how essential it is that whenever we are present with the people we are charged to serve, we need to make the most of these opportunities. It is at these times that we need to engage clients and meaningfully interact with them. They learn from us because *WE* are engaged in their lives.

Sometimes the interactions don't seem to be meaningful. We are just sitting around and talking. Maybe we're gabbing about sports. The Superbowl is the topic. We share our thoughts and feelings. They share theirs. We laugh, tease and cajole each other. The conversations seem like idle chatter. What we're really teaching is interpersonal skills. They learn new words. They begin to understand how and what we value affect our opinions. They get a chance to hear how we think. Most importantly, we get a chance to hear how they think. It's amazing how idle conversation can be a pathway to understanding the inner workings of another human being.

What is a meaningful interaction? It is being with clients and providing services with quality, with substance, as a primary component. This is what gives it integrity. This is what puts meaning into the activity. This is what leads to people forming meaningful relationships. A program that demonstrates this is one that has integrity.

Human relationships are like cables. They form by wrapping one experience around another and then another, over and over until the individual strands are meshed together. Trust is built by two human beings forming a cable that binds them together in friendship. Meaningful interaction is the way the cable is formed. Unless we are willing to spend time weaving the cable together, we won't be able to develop one. It is a two way street. Our children, our clients, the senior citizens we serve in our nursing homes must want to form the relationship, connect with us and be a part of our lives. If we understand how important it is and make every effort to provide this type of security for them, then we will find it much easier to work with them. We are only a guest in anyone's life. They must invite us in before we can be a part of their reality. If we seek to understand, to engage, to be meaningfully involved with them at every opportunity, eventually any barrier can be removed.

People Security requires that we do both parts: be with people and meaningfully interact with them. This eliminates the notion that we can spend quality time with people and that will be enough.

Now what is a meaningful interaction? Does it have to be something deep and profound? No. Sometimes, meaningful interaction is just being in the presence of another person and actively listening to him. This is often the most difficult thing for us to do, especially if we are extroverted people working with an introverted person. How many times have you met a person who is naturally reticent to talk? He seems to be listening. He just doesn't share much with you. Consider that introverted people think a lot before they speak. It is based on how they process information.

I know a particularly introverted person who tips the scales on the Myers Briggs Type Indicator. She can sit for hours and listen to me pontificate. Eventually, she may say, "My, that's interesting." I used to wonder about her unwillingness to engage in conversation. When I studied the Myers Briggs Type Indicators, it became painfully clear to me that introverts were different from me. Not better, not worse, just different. They take in information differently. They process it internally. They generally don't think out loud. They can sit for hours in the presence of an extrovert and just listen without commenting.

Another counselor friend of mine won't talk to me for months on end. Oh, he says hello, but he doesn't really converse with me. About once every six months, he comes to my office and usually begins his conversations this way. "Bert, about six months ago you said..." Then he reflects back to that conversation and replies to what I said long, long ago. The first time he did this I chuckled thinking that he'd been thinking about something I'd said for quite a long time. While he talks, I just listen. If I'm dumb enough to interrupt him and begin to engage in conversation, within minutes, I'm doing all the talking and he's listening again. Then I have to wait for another six months for him to come back. I've learned to shut up, close my mouth and open both my ears. We are good friends at work. I enjoy his company. He is a bright, articulate man, well-educated, insightful, and most of all, a free thinker. His free thinking just takes a little longer than most peoples' to find a medium of expression.

I share this with you so you can see that meaningful interaction need not be something you do. It may be more like something you don't do. This is not a contradiction. It is reality for those of us who are extroverts working with profound introverts.

People Security has direct application to families, family counseling and family preservation. Let me share with you a parable to illustrate what I mean.

The Parable of the Games

A father walks into his son's room. The son is playing a computer game. The father says, "Hey son, you want to go to a ball game this afternoon?" The son doesn't look at him. He is intent on mastering Super Mario. He says, "Nah, I'd rather play Nintendo." The father really wants to take his son to the game. He asks him again if he wants to go. The son says no. Then the son says, "Want to play Nintendo?" The father hates to play computer games. He's a sportsman. He can't understand why his son is so enamored with the Nintendo. Playing computer games makes his eyes sore. He asks the son again if he wants to go to the ball game. The son again replies, "Nah, I really don't." The father gives up. He leaves the room and walks away thinking to himself, "When I was a kid, I would've loved to go to a ball game with my dad, but he never wanted to take me. He was always too busy working out in the yard and wanted me to help him. How I hated to do yard work. Still do to this day." The father goes down to the living room, turns on the TV and watches a ball game by himself. The son continues to play Nintendo. He thinks to himself, "I know Dad likes baseball, but he knows I don't. I can't stand playing baseball, or watching it. It's so boring. Wish he would play with me." The son masters the next level of the game he is playing. He is pleased with himself and smiles quietly as the screen refreshes and he gets ready to move on to the next challenge: Level 9.

Let's take a moment to interpret this parable. The father is trying to be a good father. The son is being a son. They were interacting. The father tried to get his son to go out, do something with him. The son didn't want to go. The father couldn't understand why he didn't want to go. He was trying to do something for his son that his father didn't do with him. The son invited his father to play Nintendo, but the father refused. He doesn't like to play computer games because they hurt his eyes.

What is really going on here? The first principle, **People Security**, is not being practiced. The father was trying to meaningfully interact but on his terms. The son was trying to meaningfully interact on his terms. In this situation, neither will meet on the other's terms. Note that the father, as he walked away, was thinking about how his father never took him to a ball game. He wanted to make it up to his son, take him to games like his father didn't do with him. If we went inside the mind of the son, we might discover that he wanted to have his father sit down and play the game with him.

Now, if the father, who has experience on his side, wanted to apply the principle of **People Security**, he would've asked his son if they could play Nintendo for a while, and then go to the game. Even though he might not like to play the game, being with his son and meaningfully interacting with him on his terms, the principle would have been reinforced. Fathers who want to meaningfully interact with their children need to learn what is interesting to them and get involved in their lives. Children will learn fathers and mothers can play too. Fathers and mothers will learn children may be more apt to want to be a part of their lives when there is some common ground upon which they both meet. Playing Super Mario may not be what most parents want to do with their limited free time.

The question is: If I don't spend the time, how can I provide my son with a sense of how important he is to me? How can I make him feel secure in my relationship with him? The answer is clear. I need to engage in a dialogue with him and share my thoughts and feelings with him. Spend the time. It is an investment in the future.

Now, if the father asked the son to teach him how to play the game, the son would be placed in a new role. He would become the teacher and the father the student. Who knows, he might have enjoyed the game after awhile. Once the father and son made a connection on the keyboard, then maybe they could go to the game. The son may never have wanted to go to the game. The father may not have wanted to go either after he played Nintendo with his son. The father could explain to his son that he always wanted his father to take him to a ball game but he never did. He wanted to take his own son to a game so that he could in some small way fulfill one of his own childhood dreams. If he told his son how he was thinking and what his motives were, the son has been more apt to want to go with his father. Children will do a lot of things once they understand the reasons for doing them. Parents sometimes think their kids are mind readers. They aren't. Neither are kids able to read parents' minds. Parents and kids need to communicate their goals, aspirations, dreams, and desires to one another.

In this way, they are fulfilling the fourth principle: **Teamwork & Communication.** We'll discuss that more in a later chapter, but I'm mentioning it now because these principles are so intertwined, so easily dovetailed with one another, that once they are incorporated into a family system, amazing things begin to take place.

People Security requires that the members of a family be with one another and meaningfully interact. This means that the father learns to play with his son. He learns to do what makes the son happy and thereby teaches by example. The son learns that his father is interested in the things that he enjoys. He accepts his father on his own terms. The father accepts him on his own terms. It is not enough just to be with one another. It is important that there be some meaningful interaction occurring. When a father and a son or daughter are interested in the same things, this is an easy principle to apply. When they enjoy different things, activities and hobbies, it is necessary that each support some interest in the other. This requires effort and compromise. There is no magic involved. It means that someone will need to make an attempt to meaningfully interact.

Does this mean a parent or child must be at the whim and fancy of the other? No, by all means, No! Family members are still individuals. At times, it is essential that each participates in his or her favorite activities. What it does mean is for a family to work as a supportive, happy, healthy, system, there needs to be more meaningful interaction by choice, not by chance. Unless this principle is applied regularly, the family is not a system of people bonded together, but merely individuals who share the same spot on the earth under the same proverbial roof.

As adults, we role model for children what we hope they will become. This is the fifth principle: **Positive Role Modeling**. This will be discussed later in this text. What adults can do is be with their children and form the kind of relationship that will transcend time and space. Long after the child is gone from home and happily living as an adult with his or her own family, the memories of family life will intermittently return and the child will fondly recall the times when parent and child were bonded in a very special way.

As you can see, these principles are fully integrated. Apply one and the others are almost automatically implemented. It is a unique way to manage a system. The principles provide the foundation for a family system to be a healthy, happy, nurturing environment that supports the growth and development of all its members.

There are times when the family needs to work together to accomplish certain tasks. It is in this collaborative effort that the true nature of **People Security** becomes operational. Let me illustrate this by another parable.

The Parable of the Dresses

A daughter is preparing to go to her first dance. Her mother is excited and happy for her and wants her daughter to look her best. She remembers her first dance and how she was faced with having to wear her older sister's hand-me-down dress. This wasn't going to happen to her daughter. So, she goes out and buys her daughter a lovely dress, one that would make any young woman proud. When she brings it home and shows it to her daughter, the younger woman tries to please her mother by accepting the gift, but deep inside, she doesn't really like it. The mother makes her try it on and when it doesn't fit perfectly, decides to make the alterations herself. This will be a fun mother-daughter project, she believes. The daughter endures the activity out of respect for her mother, but would really have appreciated being consulted before the purchase was made.

The final alterations are completed, and though the dress is one that would make many young women proud to wear, the daughter is not really pleased. When the daughter tries on the dress, the mother tells her how lovely she looks.

The daughter bursts into tears and runs out of the room. The mother wonders what she said or did. She follows her daughter into her room and sits down on the side of her bed and asks her what is wrong? The daughter, with a flushed face and teary-eyes, says that she doesn't really like the dress and wishes that her mother would have asked her to come along with her when she went to buy it. The mother starts to cry too. She never thought about taking her daughter along with her. If she had done so, the dress wouldn't have been a surprise. The daughter asks her mom, "Why didn't you take me along?" The mother says, "I guess I wanted to surprise you." The daughter replies, "Well, I was surprised, but not pleasantly so. How could you do this to me?" The mother looks at her daughter and wonders what made her think that her surprise was more important than her daughter's feelings.

This is another one of those classic affairs of the heart. Mother and daughter are functioning on two different wavelengths. Mother is doing what she thinks will please her daughter. The daughter wishes that she were included in the decision. The **People Security** principle is not being applied in this situation. The mother needed to include her daughter in her plans. She would have been more successful in her planning if the daughter had been consulted. "Dear, I know you're looking forward to this first dance of yours and I want to know if you'd like to go with me to the store and pick out a dress to wear?" Now, the daughter is included in the decision and can make a decision as to what she would like to do. This is a simple solution to a complex situation. The mother wanted to make sure that her daughter didn't have to wear a second-hand dress. The daughter only wanted to be included in the decision. The fact that they both had different agendas is not uncommon.

Adults often assume that we understand what our children want. We are, after all, older and wiser, and always ready to make decisions for our children. Yet, in this parable, the opposite is true. **People Security** demands that adults and children communicate clearly. They need to share their wants and desires, their dreams and aspirations. If the mother would have told the daughter what her intent was, there is a strong likelihood that the daughter wouldn't have resisted going with her mother and purchasing a new dress. Without being consulted, the daughter was feeling left out, imposed upon by her mother. How different it would've been if the mother sat down with her daughter, told her about her first dance, the hand-me-down dress she wore, how it made her think and feel, and asked her daughter what she would like to do regarding a dress for her first official dance? This is **People Security** at work. The mother teaches the daughter how she thinks and feels. The daughter can then decide what she would like to do. This is an example of a meaningful interaction.

Some of you may say, "But isn't this really just a case of a mother trying to fulfill her childhood fantasies through her daughter?" I agree it is to a certain extent. However, **People** *Security means that we are with family members and meaningfully interacting with them.* In this parable, the mother was doing her own thing without talking to her daughter. The younger woman went along with her mother out of respect. She didn't say anything until the dress was altered and the dance was impending.

Her tears told it all. As adults, we can't make assumptions about what children are thinking and feeling. We can't assume that they know what we are thinking and feeling. It is the meaningful interaction that makes it possible for adults and kids to share both of these with one another.

When we all practice this simple but necessary communication process, misunderstandings disappear, parents and kids are more in tune with one another, and the end result is that families are not stressful places but happy, healthy, nurturing and supporting environments.

What are some of the most common ways that family members can be together and meaningfully interact with one another?

We've all heard in this day and age that dinner with the family is a thing of the past. Modern life styles aren't conducive to sitting down together as a family and eating a meal. Too many parents are working at different times and so the family is in constant flux. How to fix this? Make a date with the family and keep it. There is at least one hour a week when a family can come together and share a meal. It would be even more meaningful if the entire family cooked the meal together, then ate it and cleaned up afterward. Mom doesn't need to be the chief cook and bottle washer. Dad doesn't need to read the paper or watch TV until the meal is ready. The kids don't need to sit idly by while mom slaves over the stove. Make it a true family affair. Even the little ones can pitch in. Any activity can be more meaningful when everyone shares the work.

In my family, my father worked shifts: 8-4, 4-12, and 12-8. He was on this schedule for the 41 years he worked at the steel mill. My mother went back to college when I was thirteen and from that time on, she taught all day and went to college at night. We rarely ate dinner together after that, but when we did, it was a real treat. Dad generally did the cooking and Mom and the rest of us cleaned up. Sundays were the days we were most likely to connect for dinner.

I remember some of those meals because they were the times when we sat together, ate a meal, talked and actually acted like a family that was connected with one another. There is a need for the family to break bread together even if it is only once a week. Make it happen. Demand that it happen. Set the time aside too for discussion before, during or after the meal. Leave the TV off. Don't let football or basketball or baseball games interrupt the meal.

It goes without saying that television has adversely affected the ability for families to meaningfully communicate. Yes, watching a good movie can be a meaningful activity too. Make sure that the movie is one that all family members can appreciate and understand. In our family, we have some movies that we watch seasonally. On Thanksgiving, we watch a comedy movie called "Plains, Trains and Automobiles" with Steve Martin and John Candy. At Christmas time, we watch "National Lampoons Christmas Vacation" with Chevy Chase. We've watched these movies for years and each holiday we look forward to sitting down and laughing and sharing some time together.

The family reunion seems to exist more in the south than in the north, but there are families that strive to get together each year other than at weddings and funerals. You've all heard that before: "We never seem to get together except at these types of gatherings." Family reunions need not be the entire family. It can be just those who can attend. The reunion becomes a special time for all those who are there. It doesn't matter if one aunt or uncle or a son or daughter can't make it. The idea is to schedule it and gather together as many of the folks as possible. The family reunion is the one way to transcend generations. How can a child ever get to know his or her roots unless those roots are visible and audible to him?

How about holding a family night? Sounds corny doesn't it? But it works if you make it work. The idea is to hold a family meeting first to discuss the plan for the week. Getting the members to buy into the process is the true beginning of meaningful interaction. Once the family decides when, where, what and how, then the implementation can take place. It's important that all members of the family have some say in the process. Dad might want to go to the movies. Mom might want to go to the mall. The kids might want to go to an amusement park. There may not be any consensus until all think and feel they are a part of the process. It might be nice to brainstorm and come up with a number of possible family night activities. When the family gets a list, then it may be easier to pick one from the many. Once the family comes up with the what, then the when, where and how may be much easier to plan. The activity can be just about anything: going for a walk in a park, stopping for a custard, watching a little league ball game, planting flowers or vegetables in the garden, riding bicycles, reading favorite stories to one another, having dinner at an ethnic restaurant once a month. The list can go on and on. You're only limited by the collective genius of the family.

How about doing a family building project? Consider remodeling the kids' bedroom. What a better way to get them to clean their room than to have them organize and store all their toys and other objects before the project begins. It need not be anything that is elaborate and costly. Wallpaper is not expensive. Parents and kids really have to work together to make this a go. Let the kids pick out the colors and designs and then go at it. The excitement is in the building.

Chores are another way to get the family to meaningfully interact. Now, parents must realize that kids may not be able to do certain kinds of work. This makes for a great learning activity. Parents can use these tasks as a way to teach their children how to clean, fix, replace all sorts of things around the house. How many children learn to iron their own clothes unless their parents teach them? How many learn to cooperate and do something that is not just for them but for others as well? The opportunity to contribute to the entire family is one of the hidden agendas in this arena. When I was a kid, my mother had a neat way of teaching us about responsibility and money. She created a list of jobs and assigned a value to each one. Then, each week, we could do whatever jobs we wanted and mark them off the list. She would pay us once a week for the jobs that we did. Scrubbing the bathroom floor, toilet, shower and tub was worth twenty-five cents. In those days that was a lot of money. She wasn't concerned that the bathroom was getting cleaned almost every day. The fact that the carpets were being vacuumed more than once a week didn't upset her. Dishes were done without any arguments. Doing them was worth a dime. A dime isn't very much, but by adding up a number of dimes the dollars begin to magically appear. I could go on but the cleaning of our home was being done in a unique, creative way. My brother and sister and I were always asking Mom to add new jobs too. We suggested that cleaning the cars be added when we were big enough to take on that task. There were other things we proposed. She went along with most of them. When we got older, the money was no longer given to us because somewhere in the process, we learned that our parents would give us more money than we ever needed if we just asked for it. Now, years later, I look back on those times and realize that my ability to take responsibility for my living space was founded in these simple lessons taught by a creative mother.

Vacations are by their very nature, meaningful interactions, that is, if the family members all want to take the same vacation. The way to avoid conflict is to plan the family vacation just like you plan the family night. When children are young, they will go anywhere with mom and dad. As they get older, they want to do their own thing and the consensus building becomes more difficult. Unless a family is perfect, there won't be any perfect vacations. What I mean is that dad may want to do one activity, and mom another thing, and the kids something totally different. Time is always an issue. Money can be depending upon income. So, the solution is again to hold meetings and talk about what to do, when and how to do it. Vacations need not be full-blown trips to Disney World or the Grand Bahamas.

Sometimes it's the simple trips that are the ones the family most remembers. My parents weren't well off so we never went on weeklong vacations. In fact, we didn't take many at all. The one I do remember though was a weekend trip we made to Cedar Point in Sandusky, Ohio. We got a room in the Breakers Hotel. It was a real dive. There were cobwebs covering every corner of the room. The beds were hard and lumpy. My dad and mom laughed when I said, "Gee what a neat place," while the bellhop smiled at me. Dad pulled the two double beds together and we all slept in the "king size" bed that weekend. What makes me remember the vacation was that we all wanted to go and spend time together for the entire weekend. We laughed and played together and had a good time. We were together for three days, didn't argue with one another, swam in Lake Erie, went to the amusement park, rode amusement rides and ate dinner at a good restaurant that served excellent hamburgers, French fries and milkshakes. Vacations need not be elaborate travel agency planned events. What is important is that the family shares an experience.

Father and son, mother and daughter, father and daughter, mother and son nights out are another way for family members to be together and meaningfully interact. True, the entire family is not together in these activities, but some of them are. What can the nights out on the town be used for? Anything the members decide to do, that's what. They don't have to be elaborate activities, but they can be. Fathers and sons often will do things like go fishing or hunting. Moms and daughters can readily go shopping. The real test comes when father and daughter or mother and son plan a night out. What do a father and daughter do together? Well, for one thing, the father can take his daughter on a date. They can go to dinner, see a movie, a play, or a concert, stop afterward for a quick "drink" (milkshake and coffee) and then go on home. In the process, the daughter may just learn how a man should treat a woman on a date. The father can role model for his daughter what she ought to expect. Mother and son can do the same thing, that is, if the son can drive. But there are other activities a mother and son can do. The options are limitless. What is important here is that the family members meaningfully interact with one another. They can choose the activity, but the activity is just a venue for the application of the **People Security** principle.

People Security is an important principle in managing a family because it sets the stage for the children to grow up in a nurturing, loving, inspiring environment. Children are born, and for most part of the first 15 to 20 years of their lives, they are looking up to their parents first, and then to other adults for guidance and support.

In the communication between parents and children, many things are shared: body language, values, expectations, morals, beliefs, and most of all, unconditional love. This is one way that adults can build esteem in children. Without it, children are adversely affected.

They don't develop fully. They aren't made into whole people. What is missing is the influence of their parents on their lives.

Parenting is the one profession that requires no certificate, no degree, no license, no permission to proceed. Yet, the activity is the foundation of all cultures, all civilizations. Therefore, parents cannot enter into the lifetime relationship without some degree of commitment to be successful in the endeavor. There is always hope that life can change because we can learn new things. Regardless of how difficult family living can be at any given moment, there is hope based upon the principle of **People Security**.

At this moment, I can imagine you are wondering just how much stock a parent must invest in if he is going to be effective in the process. I believe it is essential that you as a parent invest everything. What this means is that in making children into mature, interdependent people, you've got to give it your all. A child is helpless, dependent and needy. It is our role to provide for them everything they need. This will be explored even more when we get to Principle Six that is **Dignity and Respect**. In our current discussion, it is paramount that as parents, the commitment to our children be absolute. Otherwise, it would be better that we don't enter into this relationship. It is hard to imagine, but also very true that for the first five or six years, a child's self-esteem is almost exclusively developed within the family dynamic. If self-worth is learned, then

People Security is the principle that provides the foundation for the learning to take place. Think about this for a moment. If a child didn't need parents to take care of him after birth, then he could take a credit card, get an apartment and make his own way through life.

No, life isn't like that and nor are children. As part of a family system, we are taught how to be social beings. Children are cared for so that they learn to care for themselves. They are loved so they learn how to love. They are taught how to communicate so that they can communicate their needs and wants to others. They are most of all, exposed to the primary role models in their lives: their parents. Even if there is only one parent, one is better than having none at all. The work becomes more difficult because the responsibilities are not shared. This doesn't minimize the importance of **People Security**. It would be nice to have a team approach but in the absence of a partner, the father or mother will need to assume greater responsibility.

Sometimes parents don't realize how important their role is. When they are absent from their children's lives in the formative years they are missing the most important years in which human development takes place. Children learn about fifty percent of all they will ever know in the first six years of life. In the next six years, another thirty percent is learned. From puberty on, only about twenty percent of human learning takes place. Even if you disagree with the percentages I've shared with you, the facts still hold true. Most of what we learn is completed by the age of six.

It seems reasonable and prudent that parents focus a significant amount of attention on this time period. In order to apply the **People Security** principle, parents and all adults must accept the responsibility of being involved with children in a meaningful way.

This is the initial investment. Once parents get started, they must sustain their efforts so that the children will continue to receive the kinds of support necessary to fully develop into happy, healthy, self-supporting and sustaining people.

I hope these parables help you to understand that **People Security** is not limited to only professional application. In fact, it wouldn't be a principle if it didn't have universal application.

In the human services profession, we are often charged with being in loco parentis. In the absence of natural moms and dads, we must make up for the lack of **People Security** in the lives of children and adolescents. The irony is we are paid to do this as professionals. Yet, we get bogged down in our own little worlds and don't realize just how important it is for us to go the extra mile, two or a hundred to provide this sense of security to the kids in our care. If I don't want to do this for those I'm responsible for, then I really ought to seek another profession.

I am not skilled with working with small children. I like little kids but they often confuse me. Their short attention span tries my patience. Adolescents are much easier for me to work with and so I've chosen that as my life's work. Now, you may be a person who prefers the little ones and can't understand the teenagers. Or, you may be someone who works best with adult clients. Some possess that rare and special gift of being most effective when working with our senior citizens.

For those of us who work with adolescents, we quickly learn that this age group is in the period of life where the greatest changes are taking place. They are maturing physically as they go through puberty. They are dealing with, what Eric Erikson, eminent human psychologist, described as four of the major life changes.

The most significant one is individuality versus conformity. They are often in conflict with authority. We have all experienced adolescents who treat us as if we know nothing. They act as if everything they do is unique. It is a particularly difficult period of life given the hormonal, physical and emotional changes they are experiencing.

At this critical time in their maturation, applying the principle of **People Security** is especially important when working with them. They may act like they are not listening to what we say or do, but this is a deception. How many of you have said or done something thinking the adolescents who were watching and listening to you didn't absorb anything? Yet two days later, you overhear one of them almost quoting you verbatim. They often don't want us to know that they are paying close attention to what we are telling or showing them. It's not cool to do that so they put on an air of benign indifference. At times, adolescents can be blatantly disrespectful and even aggressive. We must realize that this defiance is natural and a part of the maturation process.

For delinquents, we cannot permit them to continue to make the same mistakes they made before we began our work with them. The stakes are too high to let that happen. The consequences they are facing are not the same as the normal adolescent who is defiant but not criminally misbehaving. Our meaningful interaction with juvenile delinquents must be persistent, consistent and resistant to their defiance. They are people who have, up until this time in their lives, generally failed to make responsible decisions in some critical areas of their lives. We must reach them and guide and support them toward making responsible decisions. They need to learn to think differently, and eventually believe that their current patterns of defiance, misbehavior and criminality are getting them nowhere fast.

This is a tall order. As change agents, we face a double whammy. They are in the period of their lives when they are socially and biologically reluctant to listen to their elders. They are at a time in their lives when they really need to listen and start to think and act differently.

If they don't, the consequences can be severe. Many delinquent youth graduate to the school of higher crime and end up in the adult system. They haven't been reached. It is a tragedy when this occurs. Hence, it is essential that we practice **People Security** with them. We've got to be where they are and meaningfully interacting with them at every opportunity. This is the essence of what we are charged to do. In order to "change the world one kid at a time" we have to go to them, get involved in their lives, and begin to plant the seeds for change.

Sometimes it is disheartening to make every effort to engage a young person and he rebuffs us at every turn. We begin to think that the person is hopeless. They aren't listening or absorbing what we are trying to teach them. There is a principle that my mentor, Dr. Ken Eye, taught me more than thirty years ago when I was working with him in a maximum-security juvenile prison in Ohio. He used to say to kids who were being difficult, "I'm going to keep on talking because I don't know when you're going to start to listen." Now Ken was shrewd enough to know that when the tough kid started to talk, he'd stop and listen. Young people, even hardened delinquents who had committed serious felonies like arson, rape and murder, eventually wanted someone to listen, someone to care about them. This is the true joy of working with adolescents. They are not lost. They aren't hardened, hopeless human beings.

With the right kind of meaningful interaction, they can and will eventually begin to change their behaviors, attitudes and beliefs. This is what makes this age group so exciting. They look like adults. They want to be treated like adults. They can think and talk and act like adults much of the time.

Yet, when they are faced with responsible living, the day to day grind of being willing to accept accountability for their behavior, they often want to resort back to child-like behaviors. It is our interactions with them become more than just meaningful; they can be downright life saving.

If a particularly aggressive delinquent can use his behavior to keep us away from him for fear that he will explode on us, then he will continue along on the path to self-destruction. He will eventually explode in the wrong place at the wrong time and face dire consequences. It is essential that we who work with difficult youth realize that the client who does everything he can to keep us at bay is really sending us the most heart-wrenching form of distress signal. Yes, it is difficult to deal with this type of human being. Our natural inclination is to either fight or flee. We want to come down on his disrespectful behavior like gangbusters, or we want to flee and let someone else deal with him. What we need to do is overcome this natural inclination and wade in and work with this person. We have to overcome our flight or fight instincts, and engage in meaningful interaction with the person. We may even have to put ourselves at risk for physical harm. Anyone who has worked with difficult adolescents can relate to this experience.

Given the principle of **People Security** as a guiding light, we can proceed into the abyss that is the potentially explosive event with a sense of moral righteousness. If we don't, there is a strong possibility that this young person will not change and will eventually face more dire consequences.

It always amazes me after I've had to physically intervene with an aggressive adolescent and begin processing the incident with him, the youth and I become as close as any two persons who are not blood related can be.

The physical intervention demonstrates to the person that regardless of what he says or does, I will not be pushed away by his disrespectful, violent behavior. I must accept that this aggression is just one way the person is attempting to try to manage the emotional chaos he is feeling. Please don't misinterpret what I'm saying here. I am not condoning the way the person is acting. I am merely saying that it is a manifestation of his inability to mentally control the powerful emotional content present in his life at the present time. At the end, when we're sitting side by side on the floor and talking about what he could have done differently in this situation, I believe the most meaningful interaction is taking place. He realizes then that I truly cared enough about him that I was willing to risk injury to insure that his safety was paramount. Ever since I started working with adolescents in 1969, this has proven to be true. I would like to believe it is because of the principle of **People Security** being at the forefront of my intervention.

How much more meaningful can an interaction be than when a client is being aggressive toward others, or more tragically, himself? Sometimes, no talking will persuade an adolescent from wanting to end his or her life. The stakes are the highest they can be. At this time, flight-or-fight instincts are strongest. Yet, we wade in because we've accepted the challenge of our profession and put our personal fears aside and do all we can to preserve human life. In this case, it is the young person who may not be fully capable of comprehending what is at stake.

When hopelessness is overwhelming the youth, the escape hatch of suicide may seem like the only alternative. We step into the foray and do our best to save the person's life.

I can recall a number of situations where a person had a weapon and was going to cut his arm and I had to intervene. In one scenario, I spent 4 hours with a young man and finally got the blade away from him as he attempted to dive out a window so he could get away from me. It was a scary situation. He was waving it around and would just have easily cut me as himself. Once it was over, he was lying on the floor sobbing like a baby trying to understand how he could be so out of control. He eventually made it through the program. We were quite close after that night. I believe it was simply the principle of **People Security** being applied to its fullest extent that made all the difference.

Most interactions with our youth aren't life and death situations. They are the mundane ones where we are engaged in daily living. We often take them for granted because we don't realize how important they are. A youth is mildly resistant. We are not in the mood for it. Our tone of voice becomes sarcastic. We've got a lot of paperwork to do and we don't need any hassle. The youth realizes that we aren't interested in him and begins to be even more resistant. As he increases his resistance, we become more discontented. We raise our voice to get him to comply. The youth raises his voice too and the interaction escalates into a power struggle.

As soon as we sense that we are not meaningfully interacting but instead, reacting to the resistance, we need to regroup and get back in control. Many incidents that take place when working with difficult youth are a result of our not being tuned into the client's nonverbal communication and sometimes being oblivious as to what he is trying to communicate to us. There is a reason that people resist. It may not be easy to understand what the resistance is about and that's not the issue. It is there. The intervention becomes easier if we can challenge the youth to explain what the resistance is about. It's not important to understand why he is being resistant.

It's more critical to have the youth describe what the resistance is as if he really knows what it is. We ask him to describe it so that he can begin to understand his own thinking process. In doing this, we guide him toward responsible decision making. This is a much more pro-active way to deal with the situation.

I'm sharing this with you because it is just another example of being with a person and meaningfully interacting with him. Asking "Why" complicates the process. What does matter is that the person fully understands and appreciates that you are actively listening to them.

It doesn't matter what the situation is in which we find ourselves in. The principle of **People Security** can guide us to be successful in making a difference in an adolescent's life, whether he is a normal, law-abiding one, or a hard-core juvenile delinquent incarcerated in a secure treatment facility.

Most human services professionals don't work with clients in residential settings, let alone secure placement. Given this fact, can **People Security** serve those of you who work in community based, outpatient or mental health settings? The answer is obvious.

If we are to provide services to humans, then we need to be with our clients and meaningfully interacting with them. The outpatient setting is unique in this way. A client comes to our office and sits down and waits to be served. We take out their individual service plan and proceed to work with the client. What is prompting the client to come and see us? Is it to work on the plan or is it to get something more, something deeper?

It is my belief that what the person wants is to find a sense of security, a sense of wellbeing that we can provide him. Otherwise, he would not show up at the office. No one is forcing him to come to see us. It's not like working with the delinquent who is placed in a program by his judge.

The option to show up or not makes the need to meaningfully interact with the person even more important. It doesn't matter what the issues are. Our professional responsibility demands that we, as quality care providers, do our utmost to provide some sense of security to the needy client. Even if the client is court ordered to attend counseling services, he can avoid it without serious consequences. Judges may threaten the client with more serious consequences, but unless the client has committed some felonious crime, he won't face anything more than being chastised by the authorities. The contact we have with the outpatient client is minimal. At best, it may be an hour a week. At worst, he misses a few sessions and so we lose continuity with him. When the client is in our presence we need to insure that he receives the best possible care from us. It is essential then that we provide the client with a sense of security that his issues will receive our fullest attention. Too many times, the hour passes too quickly, the client leaves the office and we wonder afterward, "Did I do all that I could to serve my client." If we believe in and apply the principle of **People Security**, then we need not fret. Our interaction with the client will be meaningful.

I alluded earlier to the human services professional who works with the elderly. Whether it is in an assisted living environment or a full service nursing home, the need for **People Security** is present. Many older people suffer from dementia. They are sometimes passive and immobile. At times, they can be abusive and aggressive demanding from us our utmost care and understanding. Most often, they are merely sick and need to have our loving care. For those called to this continuum of human service, it is essential that the elderly experience the same sense of security that the new-born just beginning life does. Older people often display the same child like qualities too.

For those of us afraid of getting old, being around such people is sometimes disparaging. Those who choose to work with the elderly have special gifts of empathy and compassion. They possess an unqualified positive regard for those who are preparing to leave this earth for the hereafter. They know how important it is provide these people with the best care they can so they can die with dignity. It isn't easy working with the elderly because the outcome is inevitable. It is easier for us who work with children or adolescents to hope that our meaningful interactions with them will ultimately result in their developing into happy, healthy, productive human beings. For those working with the elderly, this isn't the case. It's especially important for them to have some guiding principle to keep them on track, to keep them focused, to provide them with a way to endure the hopelessness.

By caregivers adhering to the principle of **People Security**, the elderly people, like all the children and adolescents we serve, can experience a sense of security and peace. When my mother was in a nursing home for two years, I visited her almost every day. It was hard to walk down the hallway without stopping and saying hello to all the residents who were sitting immobile in their Geri chairs and reaching out for a touch, a kind word, or just a face that would smile at them. It didn't matter that many were in mild catatonic states. They could still feel the human touch, the soft, kind word, the smile sent their way. The aides and nurses are challenged in a special way. They aren't trying to change the patient's behavior, assisting them in erasing painful memories, or teaching them how to control their emotions. They are attempting to make the patients comfortable and their lives as meaningful as they can. Most quality nursing homes and health care centers employ activity directors who work diligently to provide programming designed to engage the residents in enjoyable and meaningful pastimes.

It takes a lot of time and energy to work with those who cannot do for themselves. We take it for granted when we work with young people or adults that they will be able to do most things for themselves. In the geriatric setting, the most basic functions are sometimes beyond the patient's ability to perform without assistance.

It is the greatest act of human kindness to care for those who cannot care for themselves. In the nursing home, it is the small acts of kindness that make all the difference between the environment being cold and sterile or loving and kind. It is a joy to watch the countless, meaningful interactions that occur in a highly principled home. Aides pop in and out of rooms, hold a hand, fuss over a patient's newest greeting cards, refill ice water cups, and make small talk. Emptying a patient's catheter bag, turning him over on the other side, or assisting him out of bed so that he can use the bathroom all take a lot of time and patience.

When done with love and affection, these acts dignify the final days of many people's lives. Perhaps it is the human services professional who most epitomizes the principle of **People Security**, and from these noble human beings we can learn best how to adapt it to our own work with others.

Throughout the discussion of the principle of **People Security**, I've attempted to illustrate its universal application. Many of you may be thinking, "But I already do that." I agree. Many of you do and for this, you need to congratulate yourselves. There are many who know the principle, but for whatever reason, don't apply it every day. To provide quality care, it is essential that we know the principle and apply it each and every day that we wake up healthy enough to go to our places of work and assume our human services responsibilities.

Most importantly though, let us apply it in our personal lives as well, within our families, our schools, our communities. We can make a difference in impacting the quality of life no matter where we are as we seek to serve others to the best of our abilities guided by sound principles.

PROGRAM INTEGRITY

"Providing a high degree of structure and clear expectations"

Program Integrity means providing a high degree of structure and clear expectations. Programs that use this principle demonstrate quality services in everything they do. It doesn't matter what environment in which we work: day care centers, schools, outpatient clinics, hospitals, nursing homes, residential treatment centers or secure placement. Regardless of the placement, this principle can guide our efforts to insure the highest quality care.

Whether we are willing to admit it or not, most human beings function best when they are in a structured environment. It is true that there are the proverbial free spirits who blossom and grow best when left to their own devices. These are rare specimens of the human species. Societies developed because the wanderers became gatherers and finally, farmers and merchants. Humans possess a predisposition to bond with others. Truly, society is one great program that all of us have a vested interest in and therefore, it is in our best interest to live by this principle.

How is the concept, *integrity*, defined in this principle? When we say we are going to do something, we do it. If we say we provide a high degree of structure in our work environment, then we do just that. When we say that we make our expectations crystal clear, then we do that. What we say we do, we do. This is integrity. There is no debate about it. Structure and expectations permeate our work. We live by the principle. We believe in it. We aspire to it. It is what motivates us to be all that we can be. Most of all, it is what guarantees to those we serve that our programs are designed to provide quality care.

Individuals living like hermits in the wilds of Alaska are not in any type of program. There is no social structure to their lifestyle because there are no other people living with them. The moment we add others to the equation, we have a program.

Families are the core programs that form the foundations of all civilizations. It may seem strange to consider the family a "program," but consider these criteria. The family is comprised of more than one person. The members work together in a cooperative arrangement to accomplish more as a unit than they could as individuals living alone. Each family possesses a structure that is unique. Depending how the family dynamic is structured and whether the mother or father serves as the head, the members are engaged in living in a way that hopefully, nurtures each one's personal growth and development.

Given these criteria, applying the principle of **Program Integrity** to the family is a natural fit. Families that maintain integrity are healthier and happier. When there is a high degree of structure and clear expectations for each member in the family, then all can live in peace and harmony. What this means is that each person knows what his contribution to the whole is. This may be directed by the elders, the parents, or it may be negotiated as the members, the children, mature and can be integrated into the decision making process.

How do we maintain **Program Integrity** in the family? It is mainly a function of communication. Fathers and mothers or single parents and children set in motion a process of deciding how and what each one contributes to the family program. A high degree of structure does not impede personal freedom.

On the contrary, the cooperative arrangement provides the individual with the opportunity to realize his potential. This occurs because the structure enables the individual to have the support of others as he faces the trials and tribulations of life. For years, research studies have revealed correlation between a strong family life and good health. The least healthy individuals are single men in middle age. The healthiest are married men. Children living in a nurturing family environment are more likely to be healthy. For those of us who work with troubled youth, we see the results of unhealthy family life on a daily basis. True, there are some children who experience difficulties even though they come from solid families, but this is the exception and not the rule. Please don't misinterpret this as an indictment of single parent households or alternative family dynamics. I'm sharing this as an observation. Any nurturing family, regardless of the structure, will generally produce healthy, happy offspring. A family applying **Program Integrity** as one of its core principles will be more successful in supporting the growth of all its members.

Day care centers are a model of this principle. They need to have a high degree of structure and clear expectations for all the children. The kids come from different homes, backgrounds and standards. In this milieu, the human services professional needs to clearly set expectations for the group. This insures the individuals will be able to successfully adapt to the program. Children possess a natural inclination to adapt to whatever environment in which they are. Unlike adults, children are in a constant learning mode. They haven't established their own paradigms. They are often ready, willing and able to go along with the program regardless how it is structured. As the day unfolds in a day care center, the teachers and aids can certainly provide the highest quality care if they apply the principle of **Program Integrity**.

Outpatient counseling centers are highly structured programs with sets of clear expectations for the clients they serve. People coming to receive service are scheduled by appointment. They don't show up randomly unless there is an emergency. Even then, the program that has a high degree of integrity will have protocols to deal with these situations. Most centers enter into contracts with clients. This is another way that **Program Integrity** is maintained. The contract is an agreement between counselor and client that clearly defines what each will do for the other. The individual service plan provides the foundation for the therapeutic relationship to develop. Of course, applying the principle of **People Security** certainly adds to the quality of the service being offered. Regardless of what type of service the counseling center specializes in, the application of **Program Integrity** will add to the overall quality if it is systematically adhered to on a daily basis.

Private and public schools are the epitome of systems that need to use this principle. Most quality primary, secondary and higher education systems that set clear expectations and have a high degree of structure are successful in educating their students. Those that don't have these expectations in place are often faced with strife, truancy, low graduation rates and poor morale.

Remember when Joe Clark, the famous, ball bat toting educator from South Orange High School in New Jersey, arrived to find a school in total chaos. The first thing he did was call an assembly and tell all those students who were not interested in being serious about their education and graduating to leave the premises immediately and don't come back until they were ready to do so.. He demanded the students work hard. He set very high expectations for all of them.

Clark structured the milieu in such a way that people felt safe and secure walking through the hallways and sitting in classrooms. His security force was top notch. It was necessary to re-establish control within the environment. Most of all, it was his sense of integrity about what should be taking place within the walls of that school that made the difference. Those who are familiar with the story remember that he faced stiff opposition from parents and teachers alike. The teachers who were not teaching, not setting clear expectations for their students and providing them with a high degree of structure were faced with furloughs and terminations. Those who abided by his rules adapted and overcame. The school became a model for all of New Jersey. Eventually, It was the political infighting that drove Joe Clark out of South Orange, but not before he put the school on the map.

The moral is that program integrity is essential if anyone hopes to run a quality program regardless of what service is being provided.

In the residential treatment setting, **Program Integrity** is both paramount and mandatory if the leaders and direct care workers hope to provide quality care. The more difficult the clients being served, the greater is the need for a high degree of structure and clear expectations for all who live and work within the environment.

This principle must be in effect twenty-four hours a day, seven days a week, three hundred and sixty-five days a year. Any time it is not used, residents and employees will find ways to drift away from the mission of the agency. It is always easier for people to do what they want to do than to do what needs to be done.

For instance, it's a hot night and sitting in a group room isn't something that a child care worker wants to face knowing that residents will be agitated by the heat, the tight quarters and the focus on treatment issues rather than other things. So he decides to change the structure and go out and play softball. Wrong!

We all know how inconsistency in the adolescents' lives results in their not feeling safe and secure. They will tell us that they don't like to do the same things over and over. They are easily bored and the variety is what they want. But treatment isn't about what they want. It's about giving them what they need, and a high degree of structure and clear expectations is the only way to insure that a quality service is being provided.

I recall a consulting situation from many years ago when the clinical leadership of an agency hired me to improve the quality of services in a large residential program. The issues were numerous and diverse. I spent three weeks observing the program in operation. What I noticed more than anything was the lack of structure and clear expectations. This was manifested most clearly in the group counseling being offered the clients. At that time we were doing five different types of groups. As I made my nightly rounds, what I noticed was that no two groups that were of the same type were structured in the same way. Depending upon who was facilitating the group, the process reflected the individual's own perception of how it should be structured, what the content would be, and how it was facilitated.

A particularly low point came one evening when I sat in a group and watched as the facilitator actually dosed off while the group was in session. I was appalled. For the next year, the entire system was in a highly structured process of improving the quality of its group counseling services.

Every group was monitored and evaluated. Facilitators received feedback after each group session that was based upon the structure and facilitation skills used in the group. The program embraced the principle of **Program Integrity**. It rejected the notion of a free-for-all attitude. Counselors would counsel. Clients would be counseled. Groups would be scheduled and occur on time. The structure of the groups would be the same regardless of who was facilitating them. Groups would begin and end on time. Feedback would be given and respectfully received. Everyone was charged with providing **Program Integrity**.

At first, there was a lot of resistance on the part of the direct care employees. What I was promoting demanded more work. They didn't like my being there and watching and giving them feedback. However, once the process began to unfold and the system embraced it with full support, the results were amazing. Employees began to enjoy doing groups. They set the structure in place, used effective facilitation skills to manage the groups, and gave each other feedback. What was most important though was that the youth began enjoying going to groups. Over and over, I heard them reflecting on the groups they had attended in the last day or so and sharing what they learned. Some were aware that I was the primary force in moving this process forward and did thank me. Most didn't know it and so I was able to evaluate the outcome without any bias or prejudice because I could just sit and listen to their comments.

Some nights I'd sit in as many as four different types of groups and watch with joy as the processes began to reflect the principle of **Program Integrity**. After a year, I turned over the project to the clinical leadership and went on a cross-country bicycle trip. I needed time off to unwind from the intense process I'd just endured.

The point is that unless a program is committed to **Program Integrity** and is consistently and persistently embracing and promoting a high degree of structure and clear expectations, the quality of services will be adversely affected. There is no way to sustain quality without a tenacious adherence to this principle.

Secure care adolescent placement settings and adult prisons couldn't begin to function effectively without **Program Integrity** as a core principle. Depending upon the nature of the inmate population, the structure and expectations are paramount if for no other reason than to keep the population from rioting. This is the most basic reason for invoking the principle. However, even in secure care settings for adolescents and adult secure facilities, the goal is not to just "warehouse" people. If a youth center or prison hopes to truly rehabilitate hardened delinquents or criminals, it must base its day-to-day functions on the principle of **Program Integrity**. Delinquents will eventually leave even the most secure setting and return to their own communities. While they are in the process of being rehabilitated, it is essential that the program be committed to providing them with everything they need to successfully reintegrate back into the greater community from which they came. To do less would be to violate this principle of **Program Integrity**. While in our care, we need to strive to insure that every moment of the day is geared toward their achieving this ultimate goal. It isn't good enough that a youth merely complies while in a program. This is momentary success and like a candle in the wind, easily snuffed out when the resident leaves. No, what we are after is the ultimate goal of sending responsible residents back to the community having changed their behaviors, attitudes and beliefs, and prepared to live a chemical and crime free life style and contribute to the greater good by becoming productive members of the society.

Adults facing a number of years of medium incarceration are much more difficult to deal with because of the length of their stay. It's easy to fall into habits that violate this principle. We're all aware of the ease with which prison life becomes more or less a "Mexican Standoff." Inmates in for the long haul do whatever they can to make their lives easy while on the inside. Correction officers do whatever it takes to make their lives easy while they are on the inside with the inmates who have the same goal. This is not to indict the officers as a group because this is not the norm for all. It is, sadly though, what does occur in many correctional settings. Unless a correctional facility is committed to the highest quality of care that it can provide its inmates, the normative culture will eventually reach a status quo. Inmates won't riot if officers won't come down too hard on them. If they do, inmates might riot. So, to insure that the status quo remains in effect, corrections officers don't enforce the structure and set high expectations. Change doesn't take place in the inmates because it is not the focus. This is a simplistic description of what takes place, and is being presented to illustrate a point.

Quality care, even with the most hardened group of human beings, demands that the system apply the principle of **Program Integrity**, consistently, persistently and tenaciously and fairly. The stakes in the corrections setting can be a matter of life and death. It is much more difficult to change an adult's behaviors, attitudes and beliefs than it is an adolescent's.

Their habits are more ingrained. They've had the chance to practice their manipulation skills, lying and avoidance of responsible living for a longer period of time. When thrust into a secure care milieu where there is a concerted effort made for them to do more than "dead time" their resistance will seem almost palpable.

This doesn't mean that we will back off and not demand that our programs be founded upon solid principles and that those we serve be given the opportunity to make positive changes in their lives. No, it means that if we are committed to operating quality programs and providing quality care, we are even more tenacious in demanding and encouraging our inmates to stop their past practices and prepare to return to the greater community and become productive members of society. This means we maintain a zero tolerance for violation of the structure.

This requires that we set the highest expectations first, for ourselves as the caretakers of the program, and secondly, for the inmates who are the recipients of our services. We must be compassionate and at the same time realistic and pragmatic. Adults who have been violators most of their lives are not going to undertake the change process with alacrity. It's easier for them to remain the way they are. A close friend of mine who did nine years in prison before he decided enough was enough said to me once, "I can do ten to twenty years standing on my head." What he meant by this was going into lockup was easy for him. He was so conditioned to be behind bars that he was at ease whenever he faced another prison sentence. The real struggle came when he had to return to the greater community and live a responsible life style. Then, whatever he had learned while being behind the wall manifested itself. Today, thirty one years after his last incarceration, he still struggles with some aspects of daily living, but he is free of the curse of being an irresponsible human being.

Human service professionals who work with the mentally ill know how important it is to have a high degree of structure and clear expectations for people who are functioning at levels different from the norm. Consistency in delivery of service is essential for those working with schizophrenic people.

The bipolar disordered individual needs to think and feel some measure of consistency in his or her life. Individuals functioning at low intelligence levels must receive clear sets of expectations and be cared for and nurtured in settings which provide a high degree of structure. In these settings they can realize their full human potential. If we are to provide them with a quality rehabilitation experience, we must strive to invoke **Program Integrity** in everything we do. This is what will insure quality care.

A man I know who raised two mentally challenged children spent his life applying this principle without knowing it. Every time I was with him, I was amazed at how he clearly and precisely stated to his daughter, Lisa, and son, Timmy, what they were supposed to do, how they were to act, and what the consequences were if they didn't. When Lisa would throw a temper tantrum, my friend would calmly talk to her, tell her what the expectation was, hold on to her if necessary to keep her from harming herself, and ride out the event with her in his arms when necessary. He modeled this for years and years and I'm sure it took its toll on him. His wife was not as strong in constitution and suffered from fits of depression, so most of the child rearing fell upon my friend.

He accepted it as part of his role as father and never complained. What amazed me most was his unwavering consistency. The children both loved to go for rides with him. He would drive them all over the county and show them the sights and sounds of the vast forest we live in. If they were not behaving properly, he would restrict this privilege and stay home with them and work with them until they were once again stable and ready to maintain self-control, to the best of their ability. He set high expectations for them, provided a solid, loving structure in which they could function, and did not vary it.

He wasn't a professional childcare worker. His career was in the oil and gas business and he was not college educated. What he innately knew and used to work with his two children was the principle of **Program Integrity**. To say that I admire him is an understatement.

Hospitals are the most structured environments. Protocols exist for every aspect of human care. To insure quality, to maintain standards that promote health and wellbeing, anything less would be unthinkable. I'm not sure if doctors and nurses want to see themselves as human service professionals, but as patients demand more and more humane treatment from their doctors and nurses, expecting a respectful "bedside manner," a paradigm shift is beginning to take place in these health care facilities. This epitomizes the high degree of structure and clear expectations. Patients are monitored closely to insure that recovery takes place. Charts are meticulously kept to document the delivery of service. Medical procedures are fine-tuned to meet the needs of every ill patient. Doctors and nurses take the Hippocratic Oath and abide by the principle to "Do no harm" in providing services to patients. What they do most of all is maintain **Program Integrity**. Their insistence on structure and clear expectations from the entire medical team is what can and does keep people alive. Medical errors can result in deaths. This is a simplistic description of their work, but it is accurate. It's not to avoid litigation either. It is an outcome of the highest standards they promote, the soundest principles that can be practiced in order to provide the highest quality care to the human beings they serve. They have been and will remain professionals of the highest caliber. When it is a matter of life or death, there is little room for imperfection, let alone the lack of **Program Integrity**.

The geriatric setting requires **Program Integrity** as well. Older people need and want structure and function best when expectations are clear. Just sit in a nursing home for an hour and watch how important it is for the residents to receive their meals on time, their showers, or their nurse's medication visits. Many elderly people function well below their physical and mental capacities due to their aging, but they possess a fine tuned awareness for inconsistencies in their daily lives. They are often aware of the most trivial changes in the environment. Lower the thermostat one degree, and some will be cold and others will be saying how nice it is today. It is difficult to manage such a setting where the needs are so diverse. The Alzheimer resident is a special case. Until medical science can find some way to alleviate the severe symptoms of this debilitating condition, all that will work with these people is tender loving care. When a person can no longer function in our reality, we can do little to impact their world. We can structure a program, be consistent with it and hope that our efforts are not falling on deaf ears and closed hearts.

How can a program know when it is not living by the principle of **Program Integrity**?

Sometimes assessing this can be difficult. In the complex world in which we live, structure can be present and expectations stated. What separates the wheat from the chaff is an unbiased observation of the system in operation over a period of time. To walk into a program and see something not working well, and making the on the spot assessment that integrity is being compromised does the program a disservice. It is essential that valid observations be made by people charged with maintaining a program's integrity.

Let me reflect upon my group facilitation example I shared with you earlier in this chapter. My first observations of what was taking place were disheartening. I watched one or two groups and noticed the inconsistencies in structure, the marginal skills being used and the resistance of the clients to sit through the groups with self-control and participate when asked to do so. At that moment I could have jumped to conclusions. Instead, I slowly began to gather data. I asked myself, was this a momentary set back or was this a pattern of behavior that existed within the system?

The director who hired me to do the consultation wanted me to make an immediate response to the initial report I gave him. I suggested that I take more time to observe. He wanted a more immediate response. We negotiated and I got the time. What I discovered in taking my time was that I could see the patterns more clearly. Had I set out to change the system before I thoroughly understood how to go about it, I'd have met with more resistance and a process that would have met little success. Three months after I started the observations, I was ready to invoke changes. I engaged the entire treatment team in the process and as a unified force, the change process was begun. They all clearly understood the need to improve the group process. Since I was asking them to work harder than they were before I arrived, I knew it was critical that I get their support. Basing my appeal to them on the principle of **Program Integrity**, they readily accepted the challenge. It was one of my most enjoyable professional accomplishments watching as they implemented the changes and continued to improve on the process I set in motion. A year later it was still going strong.

What made it most exciting and absolutely valuable though was that the clients said they appreciated what the clinical team was doing. Groups were much more fun now. They were learning more. They were excited about going to group. As group quality went up, acting out behaviors decreased so significantly that the director asked me if the clinical team was still holding clients accountable for their behavior. I told him to go and see for himself.

He did. What he saw was **Program Integrity** in action. The unit was physically clean. The groups were scheduled well in advance. Clients knew what the clinical schedule was and were told when they needed to get ready for group, what materials to bring and not to be late. I left the project to others for monitoring and disappeared into the sunset. He was pleased with the results. I was pleased to take a break and go and do something less stressful for a while. Since then, I've been contracted to start six new programs for that director.

I encourage you not to make hasty judgments. Take your time to watch a program operate and see where an intervention is necessary before exerting any effort. **Program Integrity** can ebb and flow with the changing of the guard. When a team loses a leader there is a natural inclination to go into a form of mourning. When more than one or two team members leave, the emotionality of the loss is compounded. This can upset the program for a period of time and yet not affect the **Program Integrity**. If the rest of the team can continue to uphold the high degree of structure and clear expectations, then the changing of leadership may not be such a traumatic experience. You have to watch and see what is really going on. Take your time. Be patient, and then when you are absolutely sure you know what needs to be done, make a surgical incision into the program where necessary and fix it with joy and respect.

How do you maintain **Program Integrity** when it seems to be working well? This is often more difficult to do because natural complacency settles into any smoothly operating system. Few people want to hear the challenge made by leadership, "We need to improve what we are doing." "If it ain't broke, don't fix it" is a common cry. No, it may not be broken, but to keep it from breaking, there is a need to monitor and evaluate the program to keep the current standard of excellence in place. This is a balancing act and requires that leadership engages the entire team in the monitoring and evaluating process. When it is top driven, it will not succeed. There is a need for all to become involved in the process. **Program Integrity** is the work of all members of the team, not just the leader. The leader may be the quarterback who calls the plays, but he can't begin to invoke the play unless the center snaps the ball. If the line doesn't block, the offense will fail. I'm sure we get the point. Make it a whole team effort. Find some interesting and enjoyable way to implement a monitoring process that is not tedious, is open to the input of all the members of the team, and serves, most of all, to improve the quality of services to the people we serve. Celebrate milestones on the way to improvement. Look for a touchstone that can serve as a reminder to all just how far we've come. Set realistic goals that can be reached. Don't expect instant change unless the program's integrity is so out-of-whack that it is essential to do major surgery. This is the area in which licensing agencies can be the most helpful. Too many program leaders see the invasion of licensing as a necessary evil. They don't appreciate that these external professionals can provide insights and suggestions that will eventually improve the program.

Yes, it most assuredly will cause more work to be done. Yet what improvement projects have you ever undertaken that don't require some effort? Sometimes it's much easier to do a little work now to avoid a lot of work later. This evokes memories of the FRAM commercial that said, "Pay now or pay later."

I remember once when our company hired Ernst and Young Consultants to evaluate our program and suggest how we might streamline it. Oh! Oh! Here it comes. Streamlining was interpreted as downsizing. They did suggest eliminating some positions, integrating responsibilities into others and rewriting policies and procedures to streamline our program. When they stepped on my toes and suggested that training do this or that, I went home that night in a rage. After a two hour walk during which I thought about all that was being suggested, it dawned on me that what they were saying would require more initial work, but would significantly improve the way we delivered our training service. I went to work the next day and immediately invoked the change. My partners thought I was nuts. A month later, all the supervisors thanked me for what I'd done.

The structure needed to be improved and the expectations changed slightly. The goal was to make the training program better. The external consultants could see it clearly whereas, I, immersed in the process, could not.

This leads me to my final point regarding change related to **Program Integrity**. It is sometimes essential to get outside people to come and evaluate what you do and offer feedback that may improve the way you do business. This doesn't mean the feedback should be categorically implemented.

No, indeed not. It does mean that you are open to it and can weigh it based upon the ease with which the change can be implemented and if it is cost effective or prohibitive. At the same time, don't let cost get in the way of truly fixing a program whose integrity is in serious trouble. If it requires money to truly make the changes and it is in the best interest for those whom we serve, then by all means, find the funding and fix it. *We can't balance the bottom line at the expense of our clients.* This would be the height of a program without integrity.

By now, I hope as you've been reading along, you can see the direct connection between **People Security** and **Program Integrity**. It is nearly impossible to have a program functioning properly unless both principles are receiving attention and are effectively being practiced by leaders and all the other employees. Unless we are spending time with people and meaningfully interacting with them, there is no program security. *It is tough to set expectations and communicate a high degree of structure to the people unless we are interacting with them by being in their presence.* As we explore the last five principles you will become more intimately aware of how intertwined they are and how, when one is not being followed, the others are affected. To use the cable analogy again, building a program that provides the highest quality care requires principles. Alone, one principle isn't enough. Bound together, they form a cable that is much stronger than the separate strands.

When quality care is the goal, it is essential that everyone commits to it. This will become more evident as the other principles are defined for you.

Step back now for a moment and consider what you've learned thus far.

Based upon these principles, how does the program you work for measure up?

Let me conclude with another parable that will help illustrate this principle.

The Parable of the Chalkboard

At the front of the classroom, there was a small chalkboard where the teacher listed the agenda for the class. At the end of each day, she would write their homework assignments on the chalkboard. Everyone was required to write down the assignment, complete it at home and be prepared to turn it in the next day. One day, the teacher was in the process of writing on the chalkboard, and her chalk broke. She tried to use the small piece that was left, but it soon wore away. She looked around the room and couldn't find another piece of chalk with which to write. Frantically, she ran to the next room to get a piece of chalk from her colleague, but the teacher didn't use chalk in her room. She came back into the room and asked the children if anyone had any chalk. None of them did. She stood quietly in front of them. The students were wondering what she was going to do now that she couldn't write on the chalkboard. She was reading their minds because she turned to the class and said, "Even though the chalk is worn out and I can't write your homework assignments on the board, you can write what I am about to tell you." She explained their assignment in fine detail. Once she was done talking, she asked one of the students to repeat what she had said to verify if he had heard the assignment correctly. "Now you all have it. Great! I'll see you all tomorrow, and I'll be sure to get more chalk." The bell rang and the students left the room knowing just what they had to do.

This is what happens when our structure breaks down and we don't have clear expectations for what should happen next. **Program Integrity** is essential if we hope to run a quality program. Chalk will wear out. If there is only one way of doing something and that way proves to be ineffective, then the integrity of the program will break down. We need to make contingency plans to insure that we can function regardless of what happens that is beyond our control.

Most of us have heard of Murphy's Law: If something can go wrong, it will. When we operate our programs with a high degree of structure and clear expectations, we are minimizing the opportunities our people have to make mistakes.

Human beings function best when they are placed in a structured setting and given clear expectations about what they are to do or not do. This is especially true with delinquent youths. They thrive on chaos and confusion. The idle time gives them opportunities to get into trouble. When we eliminate this idle time, they are more likely to remain within the boundaries set for them. Once they learn to be responsible people and capable of creating their own structure and setting high expectations for themselves, they will be on the path toward responsible living.

It is our responsibility to teach our people how to structure their lives and set high expectations for themselves. If we do this, we will be successful in our efforts to teach our people to be responsible. We need to be flexible and prepared to change as situations arise where the structure is altered by unforeseen circumstances. In other words, we need to plan for Murphy's Law and override it.

By being with people and meaningfully interacting with them, providing them with a high degree of structure and clear expectations, we are insuring that the quality of the services we provide to them are assured.

ACCOUNTABILITY, RESPONSIBILITY, HIGH EXPECTATIONS

"Teaching responsibility by expecting people to accept accountability for their behavior."

The principle of **Accountability, Responsibility, High Expectations** means we teach people to be responsible by setting high expectations for them and holding them accountable for their behavior.

All people need to learn to be responsible. The question is how best to teach it in a systematic way that insures they will fully understand what it means to be responsible?

When we're born, we are totally dependent upon others for our survival needs. For the first 2-3 years of our lives, we can't function without external care. We cry to make our needs known. If our needs are met, we stop crying. When our needs aren't met and our crying doesn't produce the results that we want, we learn new ways to communicate. The early development of human beings is a complex and arduous undertaking both for the parents and the children.

Once we begin to walk and talk and make our needs known by communicating them to others, independence begins to develop. Mind you, it's not much but it is a start. It is at this juncture in our development that forces outside of ourselves begin to teach us the principle of **Accountability, Responsibility and Expectations.**

Our parents set expectations for us to behave in certain ways. If we are wise enough to follow their direction, we may be affirmed. If we are not, we are held accountable. As we learn to accept accountability or affirmation for whatever we do, the seed of responsibility is sown within us.

This process continues throughout our early years and if we are fortunate enough to have parents who are patient, tolerant and consistent, we learn at a very early age the meaning of responsibility. I affectionately call this the **ARE of Human Development**. **ARE** is an acronym for this principle. In its simplest terms, the process never ends, but continues for the rest of our lives as we assume greater and greater control.

What happens though when there is some breakdown in the learning process? What if parents are not available to teach **ARE**? How does the child develop in a normal way if the earliest lessons in responsibility are not taught?

Some may learn this from neighbors who take responsibility for teaching them. Those of you, who, like me, grew up in a multicultural neighborhood where anyone was apt to discipline us learned that parents weren't the only people who could invoke some stiff consequences for our inappropriate behaviors. One stupid remark on my part resulted in a sharp tongue lashing from the neighbor next door. Or worse yet, Mrs. Ross, our next door neighbor and the woman I first learned was someone not to cross, would call my mother and tell her what I had done. Then I'd face double accountability. Most of the time, it was unpleasant. It didn't matter what I did, when mom or dad got wind of it, I was marched into the house and received my fair measure of justice. I never did thank her for her looking out for me. We moved away before I reached the age of reason. I did learn that she wasn't going to let me run around in her yard and be a wild little ruffian with no respect for her or her property.

Still others learn responsibility in Sunday school or some other form of religious education. This takes place long before we enter school. In this environment, the first seeds for a moral code were planted. By the time I entered kindergarten, I knew the Ten Commandments. I didn't always follow them, but I knew what they were.

If religious education taught me anything it was these primordial moral codes that are now more than six thousand years old. I might try to avoid being a good boy, but could no longer deny that I'd learned a code by which to live. My grandmother and grandfather enforced this code. I lived with them until I was seven years old.

School presented a whole new arena in which to learn how to be a responsible person. Most of us can remember being given our first homework assignment. We went home and, if we were smart, did it. Some of us had to learn the hard way and not do it and then face the consequences the next day. The ultimate accountability was the grade that showed up on our report cards a few weeks down the road.

Each year of school, every activity we engaged in as we moved closer and closer to adolescence, provided us with new and more complex lessons in how to live as responsible people. If we developed normally, most of the time we learned by trial and error. Some of us watched others goof up and said to ourselves, "That's something I won't do." Many of us did it anyway just to see if we could get away with the behavior without facing any consequences.

Natural consequences came first. These were simple learning events. Touching the hot stove burned our fingers. Climbing a tree and losing our balance and falling may have skinned our bellies or broken a bone. Run up and down bleachers enough and eventually you'll trip and fall. My first stitches came from the edge of a bleacher that I smacked my upper lip against and split wide open. I can still taste the Novocain as the doctor shot the needle into my lip to numb it before he sewed up the wound.

Imposed consequences were given almost from birth. Mom and dad would raise their voices if my behavior were inappropriate. They didn't ground me because I was too young to go too far anyway.

Disrespecting the neighbor's yard resulted in a tongue lashing, or worse, once I got home and had to face my parents. "Don't do your homework and see what it gets you." Every lesson learned moved me closer and closer to becoming a responsible person. Sooner or later, if I accepted the consequences for my behavior, I'd develop into a mature human being who could live in society without having to be monitored by others. As this process unfolded, I began to accept accountability as a part of daily living. If I kept my nose clean, like my father tried to teach me, I'd be safe from consequences. If I didn't, I'd face the inevitable.

Now, I don't believe my development was any different than yours. I only use these personal examples to illustrate how slowly the process takes place. All of us grow toward maturity at our own pace. We challenge the norms of society depending upon our own tolerance for facing the consequences for our behavior. Some learn more quickly than others. If we don't learn the lessons, we must be prepared to deal with a lot of unpleasantness.

Maturity merely means that we can and will impose consequences on ourselves. It's not pleasant to hold ourselves accountable, but if we ever hope to be responsible adults, it is essential that we learn how to do this. The locus of control remains outside of us as long as we are immature and unwilling or incapable of holding ourselves accountable for our behavior.

The ultimate expression of responsibility is the ability to tell the truth and accept the accountability that comes with it. Those who learn this lesson develop into responsible adults. Those that do not live responsibly often face dire consequences for a significant period of time, sometimes well into their adult years.

There are the unfortunate few who never learn to tell the truth, never to accept accountability for their behavior and are sentenced to face years behind bars as a consequence. They blame others for their condition. They shirk responsibilities when assigned, and spend a lot of time in the principal's office, attending counseling sessions, being assigned a caseworker when they are truant or incorrigible and earn the label, "juvenile delinquent" when they commit felonious crimes. They may end up in a treatment program or secure placement if they are particularly resistant to change or aggressive toward those trying to guide and support them.

It doesn't matter what their age is, the lessons remain the same. **ARE** is always in effect. Every action we produce has some consequence. If the behavior is appropriate, say we work hard and produce goods for our employer, we get a paycheck. Our behavior is affirmed with money. We like it and so continue to work. If we don't work hard, produce little, slack off and do as little as possible unless our boss is staring over our shoulder, then we may face a furlough, or worse; we might be fired.

How many of you can recall your first paid employment? I was a paperboy. A real entrepreneur! My route covered ten miles and I was responsible for delivering sixty-seven papers a day, six days a week. I got my papers at my home. Then, I'd get on my bike and race around my small town delivering them.

At the end of the week, I collected money from my customers and had to then pay my bill. Whatever was left over I got to keep. It was a complex business for a ten year-old to manage. Some people paid every week. Some paid every other week. Then, there were those who paid for a month in advance.

Now, I had to learn how to budget my money. No matter what I did or how I manipulated my money, once a week I had to pay my bill. If I spent too much one week, the next week I might run short. There was no credit with the paper. You paid the bill or you lost your route. It was as simple as that.

I share this story with you as a classic example of the **ARE** process in effect. The expectation was that I deliver my papers on time, in good condition every day. As long as I did that, my customers would affirm my good work by paying me. When they paid me I could pay the newspaper. If I paid the newspaper for the papers, I was rewarded by keeping my route. If I kept my route, I could continue to earn money. The money I earned was my own. I could blow it, or, if I were a true entrepreneur, invest it in something. I rarely did, but I could have done so. For three years, I delivered papers regardless of the weather, my health, or my state of mind. When I finally quit, I missed the steady income. This is another example of ARE. If you don't work, you don't have any money in your pocket.

When people seek out our services or are assigned to us to receive some sort of counseling or more serious interventions, we are placed in the position of being the locus of control in these people's lives. For those who are not in the human services profession, this assignment might appear to be a dubious distinction. We know how serious it is to be charged responsible for another human being. Since we have demonstrated responsibility in our own lives, we are paid by others to take care of those who are not as responsible.

At this point in my life, I'd much rather work with people than to deliver papers and be subject to the whim and fancy of my customers. It's nice to get paid regularly and the same amount every two weeks.

Accountability, Responsibility and High Expectations alive and well inside of me. This principle doesn't go away when we get older. It becomes even more serious as we trudge on into adulthood. Since it is, I can easily believe in it and teach it to others. Unless I weren't living it, I would be a hypocrite if I tried to teach it to others.

Who can say when the lesson is finally cemented within our psyche? Was it at the end of the first week when I got my first paycheck and smiled all the way to McDonald's to buy 5 burgers, 10 fries and couple of chocolate shakes and plunked down my profit for the week, a cool $2.43. We each need to assess our own ARE and decide when it finally took root. Those who don't get the point, face a lot of hard times.

One of the natural consequences of not working is that no one is willing to give you credit. If you work hard and pay your bills, you get all the credit you want. Try to take the easy way through life and eventually the consequences begin to pile up.

It amazes me at times when I'm working with a youth who's been in five or ten programs, they still don't get the message. Some responsible adult, a probation officer or a judge, sees some value in investing in a particularly difficult youth and spends a significant amount of money trying to get him to learn to be responsible. The youth continues to try and do it his way and the results are always the same. This person arrives at my doorstep.

Teaching a client to be responsible begins by setting high expectations for him. No person rises to the level of responsibility by making excuses for less than responsible behavior. How many times have you worked with a child or youth and the parents defended his behavior, made excuses for it, and tragically, but not often, actually blamed themselves for their child's condition? Up to a point, parents are responsible, but after the age of reason, a child must accept responsibility for his life's condition.

My wife teaches first grade. She tells me interesting stories about how her children are already testing the limits with her. They are a ripe old age of six or seven. For them to test the limits, they must know what the limit is. All children and adolescents will test limits. This is normal development. Concern arises when the child or adolescent doesn't internalize this message: You are responsible for your own behavior. This is the challenge for all families, human-services agencies, prisons, hospitals, health care centers and nursing homes. From birth to death, as I pointed out earlier, **ARE** is in effect. How we get the child, youth or adult to learn this and finally accept it is the real challenge.

The parent who defends or makes excuses for his irresponsible child is enabling him from becoming a responsible adult. We don't like to be embarrassed by our children and would much rather tell stories about their successes than have experience their failures. To insure that the failures are minimal, we need to teach them to accept accountability for their behavior by telling and showing them that they are responsible for their behavior.

It is much easier to reinforce ARE in a residential placement setting than it is in an outpatient counseling, day treatment program or the family. Sometimes it seems nearly impossible to successfully convey the message at home. One of the strategies that works well when doing consequence counseling is to ask the child or adolescent who needs to be held accountable for his or her behavior, "What are you going to do to clean up the mess you just made?" Now the mess isn't spilling his milk on the table. No, I'm referring to the mess created by being irresponsible.

What I've noticed is that most adolescents will eventually design consequences for themselves that are much more punitive than I could devise.

I don't let the client leave my presence until he has clearly stated what he is going to do, how he's going to do it, when it's going to be done, and what he has learned in the process. This insures that the intervention I've made is pointing him in the direction of responsible living. What is enjoyable about this type of intervention is that the client gets the opportunity to accept accountability for his behavior and at the same time, design it, too. This is a double lesson in responsible living. By his designing his own task, he takes on the majority of the ownership for the behavior and the consequence. I can honestly say that I've rarely, if ever, had to return to the client and get him to finish his clean up. The reason is obvious. He owns it the minute he designs it. To not do it would be to demonstrate that he is not responsible. By designing it, he is saying to me, "See, I can be responsible." Yes, I do hold him to it. I'd be less than responsible if I didn't. Let me share with you what I consider to be the most important questions any human services professional can use to guide people toward responsible living. I've used a couple of them above, but let me list them here.

The 5 Key Questions

First, ask: **"Who's responsible?"**
When I am intervening with someone, I ask this question to establish that he realizes who is responsible. If the person sarcastically says, "You are," I ask it again. I'm not going to get engaged in a verbal power struggle. I may ask this question a dozen times until the person finally, says, "I am."

Once this ownership is established, then I will proceed. This question parallels the first step of AA. It helps the person break through the denial of who is responsible for the behavior. As long as the person is pointing the finger elsewhere, there is no chance for growth and development to take place. Sometimes a person will say, "I don't know." The response to this is simply, "Well, who's responsible for knowing?" This further reinforces the need to take responsibility for everything in one's life, including knowing. Rarely have I found a person who doesn't know what is in his best interest. Never have I found someone who eventually doesn't admit that he is responsible. The reason for using this "I don't know" routine is to avoid being responsible. It's as simple as that.

The second question is: **"What are you going to do that is in your best interest?"**

This immediately challenges the person to begin to do something to change what he is doing. This is an action step. It's not important for us to understand why a person is acting in a certain way. What is more important is to engage the person in doing something that moves him toward action. Talking about doing something isn't the same as actually doing it. If a person say, "I don't know," I simply state, "I don't know isn't an answer." I repeat the question, "What are you going to do?" This pattern of inquiry will continue until the person says what he is going to do. Now he is two steps down the new path toward responsible living.

The third question is: **"How are you going to do that?"** This question guides the person toward assessing the action he is considering. It asks him to consider what the action will produce. You might say, "What good is this?"

It is action that hasn't taken place yet so what is the reason for stopping the person from just proceeding?

This question prompts the person to think before he acts. It is an interim step that helps a person to consider as many of the possible consequences. Some of you might see this as consequence counseling and you're right.

In order for people to learn to be responsible, we need to do consequence counseling as part of the change process. It isn't a magical process. There is work involved in getting people to move toward responsible living. Repetition is often necessary. Further inquiry results in the person learning more. Until the person makes a decision that is in his best interest, the inquiry continues.

The fourth question is: **"How is that in your best interest?"**

This question is asked when the person proposes doing something that has a marginal chance of success and, if enacted, the consequences may be less than pleasant. Now, rather than judging what the plan is and giving the person my opinion, I am asking him to do another level of assessment. This thinking about the thinking is called *meta-cognition*, and often results in a much deeper level of understanding. Once the person assesses the plan in more detail by asking himself this question, he is ready to act. The individual's commitment to the plan that is finally decided upon by the person is much deeper when it is clear that the consequences are not unpleasant ones.

Sometimes, I combine questions 2 and 4 in this way, **"What are you going to do right now that is in your best interest?"** This makes the person really stop and think and invokes the concept of "best interest" into the thinking process along with the possible action the person is considering. any times when I have been teaching these questions, human service professionals stated that they liked this combination of the two and can see how using it could speed up the change process.

I could call it the fifth question but would rather leave them separate and let you use them in whatever combination you choose.

Finally, before the person leaves my presence, I ask the final, integrating question which is: **"What did you learn?"**

I'm not willing to let the person leave until I'm sure that he learned something new. What is more important is that they are able to learn something right now that can be used later in another situation. If the person says, "Nothing," I ask the question again. I'm not willing to let the person give me the "okey-doke." I might say to him, "*Nothing and nothing equals nothing.*" The person needs to learn something and I'll pursue this inquiry until there is a clear statement that something was learned. I'm looking for at least three new ways, options or choices the person can use to behave differently in the future. The reason I want at least three is so that the person can then see the way he was acting in this situation was limited to one choice. By being limited to only one, the person cannot really move to a higher level of responsibility. The more choices a person possesses to manage his or her life, the greater the chance is he will be more effective in living responsibly.

These questions are designed to challenge people to think about responsible living. Many times, counselors, teachers, and caseworkers fall into the trap of giving their clients or students the answers, opinions, and suggestions on what to do. If I give advice to a person and the person accepts it and finds that the advice worked, who gets the credit. Yes, I do. I did the work. Now, if I give advice to a person and the person uses it and the advice backfires, who gets the blame? Yes, I do. In either situation, I get the praise or the blame.

Quite frankly, I don't need either. I can manage my own life and don't need praise or blame from others. We are charged with teaching our people how to be responsible human beings. To do anything that impedes the learning process is contrary to our mission. In the standard practice of giving advice, the person is left out of the decision making process. We're doing the work for him. We give the advice because it's easier than challenging the person to think for himself. The inquiry process takes time and practice. It is easier in the short run to just give advice. In the long run, the person who is thinking is learning how to manage his own life. In this process, our role is to prompt learning. We are guides and supports. We aren't the helpers. The person is doing the work, the thinking. We are merely catalysts in the change process. Once he begins to make responsible decisions, we become unnecessary.

A more practical reason for using this inquiry process is that it frees me from taking responsibility for the other person. I don't want to be responsible for others if I can help it. No, this doesn't mean I won't take responsibility for someone else if they can't, are unwilling to do so or if a life is at stake. What I mean is that I don't want to make decisions for others. I want them to make decisions for themselves.

This radically changes the counselor-client relationship. This places me more in a role of teacher and mentor rather than a helping professional. Sure, teachers help, but they do so by teaching people to help themselves. I don't want folks to be obligated to me. I want them to be happy and healthy and control their own lives. To that end, I use inquiry to move them along the path of responsible living using the questions to guide their growth and development.

How easy is it to teach these questions to a person? I maintain it is much easier to spend a year trying to teach a person to be responsible than it is trying to assess why they aren't. There is a paradigm shift occurring in the helping professions. We are moving away from psychotherapy and toward psycho-education.

This means that we aren't as concerned about what caused the problem in a person's life. We are more concerned that the person understands how he is put together. We want him to learn how to use whatever knowledge, skills, abilities, talents and character traits he possesses that can help him to manage his own life in a way that works for him. This frees him from dependence upon others and eventually eliminates the need for external support of any kind. He will know how to manage his life responsibly because he has tools that he can use to guide him.

I've taught the *5 Key Questions* to counselors, clients, and most importantly, use them to manage my own life. I think that the best example of their applicability can be illustrated by their use in a group setting working with MH/MR adolescent girls.

I was invited to do some consulting work for a mental health program in a city away from my own program. I was excited about the opportunity to share some new ideas with a program that was struggling with effectively intervening with its clients. After working with the clinicians all day, I was asked if I could cover the floor while they met to decide how to implement what I'd taught them. I said sure, and asked the director's permission to run a group with the girls and teach them what I'd taught the clinicians.

She said, "Be my guest." Group work is always fun for me. It is the most efficient way to teach a lot of people concepts and principles.

I asked the girls permission to share some new ideas with them. I guaranteed them that what I was about to teach them would profoundly affect the way they managed their own lives. This challenge piqued their interest and I was off and running. I taught the questions in much the same way I did to the clinical team. I used some activities to engage the girls in personal problem solving. When I was nearly finished and they were excited about trying out what they had learned, I noticed that one girl was being very contemplative. I asked her what she was thinking. This was our dialogue.

Parable of the Group

Girl: So what you're saying is that if I accept responsibility for what I'm thinking or   feeling, then I don't have to feel bad or good or anything. It's what I choose for myself?
Bert: That's about it.
Girl: But that is really hard to do. I mean, you're saying that if someone steps on my   toe, I don't have to get upset. I can just look at the person and say, "Hey, that hurt. I don't appreciate your stepping on my toe."
Bert: You got it.
Girl: But that's not easy to do.
Bert: I didn't say it was easy.
Girl: I can see the value in doing that, practicing that. But it won't be easy.
Bert: No it won't, but what is the alternative to not doing it.
Girl: (Thinking for a moment). The alternative is that I get upset and want to go and   hit the person. Then I'm really in trouble. That's not cool.
Bert: So what are you going to do that's in your best interest?
Girl: You're doing it right now.
Bert: Yes I am. It's a habit with me.

Girl: But that's hard to do.

Bert: I never said it would be easy.

Girl: But I can see how if I learned to do this, I'd be a much freer person. I wouldn't be getting upset over stupid things. I'd be in control of me.

Bert: Yes you would.

Girl: I like that idea. I want to be in control of my own life.

Bert: I would prefer you be in control too.

Girl: Bert, you're an old man. It's easy for you to do this. I'm 14 years old. It's not easy to do what you're asking me to do.

Bert: I didn't say it was easy. But imagine for a moment that you practice these skills   for two years and by the time you're 16 you'll be fully in control of your life. You   will know who is responsible and decide how to act based upon what's in your best interest. No one will need to think or act for you. You will be your own person and you'll be a wise, mature, happy, healthy sixteen year-old with your whole life ahead of you.. But it's your choice. You do what you think is in your best interest.

Girl: I've got to practice these for myself then. I like being in control, being responsible.

Bert: I'm sure you do.

Girl: You make it sound easy, but it's not.

Bert: It's not easy at first, but with practice, it becomes second nature to you.

Girl: How long are you going to be here?

Bert: Just today.

Girl: Well, thanks for coming and teaching me something new.

Bert: You're welcome.

2nd Girl I think you're crazy.

Bert: Some have said that to me before.

1st Girl: Why are you being disrespectful? Bert isn't disrespecting you.

2nd Girl: Because it's my choice. I will accept the consequences for being disrespectful. I'm in control of my own life. (She starts laughing).

1st Girl: Why don't you grow up?

2nd Girl: Because right now I think it's in my best interest to act my age which is 13 and you can't make me do anything. I'll accept the consequences for my behavior.

Bert: You got it (To the second girl)

2nd Girl: I know, but I thought I'd just like to have some fun with you.

Bert: Have all the fun you want. You know who's responsible.

2nd Girl: Grrr......

The group ended and we all went outside to play basketball, practice cheerleading routines and just sit in the warm sun. What a fun day we had together.

I share this with you as a simple illustration that no matter who you are working with, there is value in teaching people how to use these questions to manage their own lives.

When I hear clients saying to each other, "Hey, do what's in your best interest," I know the seeds for responsible living are planted and beginning to grow.

In the secure placement setting, the same strategies apply.

Accountability, Responsibility, High Expectations is essential in treating the most violent adolescent offenders. They need to receive a steady dose of it each and every moment they are in our care. In many states, the balanced and restorative justice initiative is being implemented. This is a paradigm shift away from punishment and moving toward retribution. They are teaching residents that their criminal acts are not crimes against society, but crimes against people.

Consequence counseling takes on a whole new dimension when the resident begins to accept that his behavior doesn't take place in the proverbial void. His criminality takes on a new meaning for him when he is constantly reminded that by stealing a car, he victimized: a family of four people, a police officer who missed his daughter's final senior basketball game, an insurance adjuster who was called out in the middle of the night because of the family's need for a vehicle, and the resident's parents who are wondering what it's going to take for him to once and for all stop violating society's laws. This movement in juvenile justice is bound to have an effect on the youthful offender. If he internalizes how the crimes he commits are effect real people, he may begin to change his thinking. This is a difficult lesson for most hard core juvenile delinquents to accept and internalize. They will often deny it for months or even years. I remember a client who had a perverse way of rationalizing his pathological stealing. He said, "If I steal from a house with no one in it, I'm a petty thief, but if I have the courage to go into a house and rob it when someone's home, I'm cool." For some strange reason, his thinking was really warped. He saw his act as courageous, I guess, because he was taking a risk in committing his crime. By stealing from a house where no one was home, he was not demonstrating courage. He was in the program for more than a year before he started to unravel his convoluted thinking patterns.

Programs that want to insure quality care must institute this principle if they are   to teach their clients to accept responsibility for their behavior. This is almost purely a cognitive approach to effecting change in others. It doesn't matter why the child or juvenile did what he did. It only matters what he is going to do differently now to stop being a victimizer.

For years, human services professionals took a "bleeding heart" approach to treating children, youth, and delinquents. What we've learned is that it rarely works. The reason is simple. In assisting a client to understand what made him commit such acts, the counselor inadvertently was providing him with an excuse for his or her behavior. What matters most is his accepting responsibility for his behavior, not why the behavior was done. Yes, it's tragic that some children have parents who are in prison, or no parents at all. It's horrible that some children and adolescents have been physically or sexually abused, or even worse, both. We could catalogue the horrors done to children. This doesn't change what has happened. Nor does it change what the client did. Today is today. What happened yesterday is purely personal history. What happens tomorrow is only a promise. The focus is on the here and the now. The question is: "What are you going to do right now to stop being a victimizer and begin to live a responsible life style?" In this approach, the client must focus on his behavior and thinking. Excuses are out. Taking the victim role is unacceptable. He can't invoke the thought that because his parents weren't good role models, he grew up this way. Our response is this: "No, sorry, young man. You are old enough to make choices. You can and will learn to be responsible or you will continue to be reminded of how your behavior is affecting a whole lot more people than just you." By making such a statement we are taking the wind out of his excuses.

I'm sure that you can see the effectiveness of such an approach. It cuts to the chase. The child, youth or delinquent is required to accept accountability for his behavior. The expectation is clear: *change or continue to face dire consequences*. There are no excuses. There is only change.

Sometimes, to emphasize the seriousness of the condition the client is in, I'll do my group on "The Three Choices." What I teach the youth is that there are three choices he can make if he continues to pursue the current life style. The choices are prison, death or change. In all the years I've taught this seminar to delinquents, I've never had one choose prison or death. As soon as the choice for change is made, I state to the group, "Now that you've made that choice, everything you do will be pointed toward change. When I intervene in your life and address your behavior, I'll be reminding you of this moment when you made the commitment to become a responsible member of society."

There may be some readers who are appalled by my taking this no nonsense approach to change. I can assure you that it is not done to insult or make him feel badly. It is done so that he begins to think about his behavior in rational terms and accept that the acts committed effect everyone, including him.

This is a radical departure from client-centered therapy and some of the other modalities where emotional content is the primary focus. If these worked with our types of clients, we'd use them. What works is changing the thinking that leads to the behaviors that result in victimization, arrests and loss of freedom. I like to use the Descartes concept with a new twist. "I think; therefore, I'm free." When a client is on automatic pilot, he is apt to get into trouble again. For the rest of his life, monitoring the thinking process will be a life-saving activity. This is the cognitive behavioral approach and is the most effective one to use when working with difficult youth. (See, I Think: Therefore I Am, by the same author).

In the adult corrections setting, the focus on **ARE** takes on monumental proportions. Due to the fact that adults are much more habitual in their behavior, it becomes essential to force them to focus on their thinking and how it has caused them to live outside the boundaries of responsibility. Years of conditioning have led to the criminal's current state of being. Only hard work and commitment to changing the thinking will begin to prepare the inmate to return to the community with any chance of remaining free. He must begin to face the world with an open channel of communication. What does this mean? He needs to be open to feedback, take risks at self-disclosure, be highly critical of himself, his thinking, and willing to face the self-disgust that is necessary for him to stop doing what he has done to himself and others. Secondly, he needs to analyze his automatic thinking errors and apply correctives. For instance, when a criminal starts to blame others for his predicament, he must stop and accept responsibility for being in prison. He alone was the cause, no one else. There are a host of other errors that are consistently made and each one needs to be addressed. Finally, the criminal must start developing automatic deterrents to committing any more crimes. The fear of getting caught again isn't enough of a deterrent for the criminal to stop his behavior. No, the criminal must work and work on his thinking. He must make moral inventories. Eventually, he will descend into pure self-disgust and finally come to realize that to lie, cheat, steal, rape and murder are all wrong. Wrong! To even think about committing the crime is to already have done it. It's like the passage from the Bible, "He who lusts after a woman already has committed adultery in his heart." This is true for the criminal and his behavior. He cannot even think about it because in so doing, he is getting excitement from it. This is a radical way to approach the change process, but without applying this principle, there is no chance that the criminal will return to the greater community and become a productive member of society.

Most secure care facilities are not treatment oriented. They hold inmates, provide some recreation for them, feed, clothe, shelter them and make them work. For the inmate facing life in prison, there is little need to focus on rehabilitation. However, for the inmate doing time for a car theft or dealing narcotics, he will eventually be released. Unless some intervention is done while the inmate is incarcerated, the likelihood of his returning to the community and committing another crime is high. It isn't enough to just punish a person for his crimes. There is a need to truly intervene and break the cycle of criminality. Teaching an inmate to accept accountability for his behavior and ultimately become a responsible person is the only way to insure that he will have some chance to make it once his time is served. Some will resist just because they believe being responsible is hard work and boring. Yes, it's sometimes boring being responsible. What causes people to pursue a life of crime? It's not the spoils. It's the excitement. To be a responsible person is not as much fun because it isn't as exciting. This is the way the criminal thinks. We need to teach him to think differently. Yes, being responsible is sometimes boring. However, the responsible person is also free. The more responsible a person is, the freer he is. The most irresponsible people in the world are facing life in prison without parole. Like it or not, accepting and living by ARE is the one true way to provide quality care in the adult prison environment.

It doesn't matter what the milieu is. This principle has universal applicability. All human beings need to learn **ARE**. First, we have to learn it so we can teach it. Then, we have to teach it or we aren't really providing quality care. Some might argue that youth in a mental health program who possess limited coping skills, might have a hard time understanding the principle and applying it to their lives.

We must believe that all people can learn to be responsible. Some might take longer to learn it, but eventually they can be taught. What often happens is this. If, after a few attempts to teach the principle the inmate fails to internalize it, we stop teaching and determine that the inmate just can't get it, he certainly won't. Most of the time, learning is based upon repetition. We must do something over and over again before we get it. How many of you remember someone's name after the first time you are introduced to him? Most don't, I agree. I know it takes me three repetitions to get it. Once I've associated a name with a face three times, it's locked in place. The same holds true for learning to be responsible. The issue is that learning **ARE** is much more complex than learning someone's name. We've got to be patient, persistent and persuasive (P-3) if we are to succeed in teaching **ARE** to the mentally challenged person. It took my friend, Harry, many years to teach Lisa and Timmy to be responsible for their own behavior. They never fully learned **ARE** because of their limitations. They did learn it to the best of their ability. This is all that can be expected of people with limited abilities.

In the health care facility or nursing home, **ARE** fits well, too. Even though many elderly people suffer from short term and some long-term memory loss, they can still take care of themselves. They may be suffering from any number of ailments, but there is a need for them to still be responsible for themselves. If that is not physically possible, then we must intervene and care for them. But if it is possible, then we need to encourage them to be as responsible as they can for their day to day needs and wants. By encouraging them to retain as much responsibility for themselves as possible, we are insuring that they maintain their human dignity.

As you've been reading this description of **ARE**, have you noticed that it would be nearly impossible to teach someone to be responsible if you weren't with the person and meaningfully interacting with him, and if you weren't setting clear expectations within the structure of your program? In other words, **Accountability, Responsibility and Expectations, People Security** and **Program Integrity** are interdependent upon one another. One can't shape a program if the other two aren't present. If two are being used and the third is not, then there will eventually be a breakdown in the quality of service being provided to the people being served. The real beauty of these principles is that as each one is improved, the entire program is improved. Yet, if one isn't working well, six other principles are still supporting the system. Lastly, by using them, a program has a built in way to measure its performance. If someone knows these principles he can walk into the program and see and hear if they are being used or not. From the observation, he can tell what needs to be done to improve the system. Quality care is the outcome.

TEAMWORK AND COMMUNICATION

"Working together and effectively communicating with one another"

Teamwork and Communication means working together and effectively communicating with one another.

Of all the principles, this is the most difficult one to consistently apply philosophically and practically. It's not that it is difficult to understand. No, it is very easy to do that. What makes it hard to achieve is the context in which we exist. Let me explain.

The historic American lifestyle is one of rugged individualism. Our predecessors came to this land to escape religious persecution. They wanted to live where they could be free from tyranny. What they discovered was a land that represented its own tyrannical forces. Undeterred, they sought to tame the land, the native people, the wild animals, rivers, forests and anything else that got in their way. In the process of developing a great nation from "sea to shining sea" they indoctrinated all of us to be independent spirits, free of boundaries, able to leap tall buildings in a single bound, achieve more, live faster, and sadly die younger.

I'm exaggerating a little here, but you are very much aware of the essential nature of the culture in which we live. Add to this a highly competitive nature that is fostered as early as age one when our parents brag about how fast we crawled and then walked and how many words we said, you can see what is coming.

Our schools trained us to compete for grades and positions on sports teams. Grades, sports, popularity, dress codes, school activities and leadership positions taught us to go and do more, be better, run faster, look cooler, all as part of the preparation for going out and competing for jobs in some profession, business or industry.

We go at it with gusto, and then, when we're off, we continue to compete in softball leagues, bowling, golfing, and a host of other activities that continue to hone in us the competitive edge.

What happens during all this conditioning is that we become extremely adept at competing. It is part of our culture, and the thread by which our social fabric is woven. It's neither a good or bad condition. It just is. Simple and to the point, America is a competitive society.

Now, we are smitten with ourselves. We enjoy what our competition has earned for us. We praise and laud ourselves for our successes. Ah, but here is the rub. When we go to the human service work place where profit is not the ultimate goal but quality services are, competition doesn't necessarily serve us. It is not what produces a healthy patient, a sober client or a responsible inmate. Competition truly impedes teamwork and communication among caregivers. It stifles communication. It is a burden, not a blessing. Some might even say it's a curse.

Navy Seals are one branch of the military that epitomize **Teamwork and Communication**. Their training is the finest in the world. They pride themselves on never having left a fellow Seal behind on any mission. What does it take to develop the level of teamwork and communication the Seals achieve?

First of all, what about a year of intense work with nobody but your own team? Imagine what it would be like to enter the program you currently work for and be told that for the next year, the only thing you will be doing is training to work with your team. You won't even be going home. You'll be training twenty-four hours a day, seven days a week for three hundred and sixty-five days.

How does that sound to you? Add to this regimen, intense physical, mental and moral conditioning that breaks ninety-seven out of a hundred people. Want more? Then, when you're done with your training, we'll place you in the most severe conditions a human being can face and you and your team can do your thing. I'm sure that most of you are cringing right now. I can't imagine being in water for more than a few minutes, let alone for hours on end, in pitch darkness and navigating through the underwater world with only an illuminated compass strapped to my wrist. JAWS may have been a movie, but it's real to me.

We will never achieve that level of teamwork and communication but that's okay. We're not generally going to be placed in life and death situations like Navy Seals are. We are going to have people in our care who are facing life or death if they don't change some of their behaviors, attitudes or beliefs. Every human service milieu has its own share of tragedies that reinforce what I have just said. We enter the profession to change lives, to make the world a better place for people to live, and still, there are those who don't make it. What keeps us going despite the fact that we know someone with whom we are working is not going to be successful, is going to fail, and perhaps die?

I remember going to a funeral of one of my clients on my last caseload. A few months before, we hunted deer together. Andy was a fine young man. As far as I could determine, he was making it in his own way. Then I got the call that he was dead. The circumstances under which he died were sketchy. It didn't matter anyway. He was dead. This was the only reality that mattered to me. As I stood by his casket and looked at him, I asked myself, "What more could I have done for you?" I struggled with this question for a long time.

My final conclusion was nothing. He was free. He had the power to choose. What prompted him to drive a car under the influence of a chemical would never be known because he wouldn't ever again come to ongoing therapy group and work on his issues. I said goodbye to him and went back to work thinking to myself what my sponsor always told me, "Where there's breath, there's hope," meaning that I needed to focus all my energy, concern and love on those people in my care who were still breathing. Those who were no longer breathing would only drain my energy if I let them. I vowed I would never let that happen. So, our work is about life and death. We know it can come, so we work as hard as we can to keep that from becoming a reality for our people.

An AA Principle states, "We alone can do it but we can't do it alone." It applies directly to the principle of **Teamwork and Communication.** There are too many people who need our guidance and support and most of us are not willing to work around the clock to keep those we serve from ending up the way Andy did. When we realize and accept this as a condition of our work, we can then turn off our egos, our competitive edge and function as a team member. Whether it is a clinical team, a teaching team, a family team, a medical team, the team comes first. I come second. When I get in the way of the team's effort, the people we all serve receive less than quality care. This is a very difficult principle for most of us to follow. We often pay lip service to it and say we understand what it means. What is hard to do is suppress our egos and do what is in the best interest of the team. Unless we're Navy Seals, we haven't been trained to work with one another. Our competitive spirit gets in the way.

We are individuals. Yet, as teams, we need to support the personal expression of our skills, talents, knowledge, gifts and wisdom. What we must do is find a way to use all of these individual talents in such a way that they support the overall teamwork and communication that is vital to achieving our mission.

This makes me think of the Oakland Raiders. For years, they have had more Heisman Trophy winners on their roster than any other NFL team. Yet, year after year, they perform marginally because superstars are difficult to harness into a cohesive team. They possess extraordinary talent, but they have a hard time working together and placing the team before self and the achievement of personal bests. The same holds true for programs where there are many talented individuals who all think they know the best way to do things. They are all superstars. What they haven't learned is to work toward the common good.

Building a team and learning how to effectively communicate with one another takes a lot of work. Unlike the military that spends ninety-nine percent of its time training for the one percent of the time when it may be called into conflict, programs spend just the opposite amounts of time. We are providing service ninety-nine percent of the time and only one percent is devoted to training. We generally learn most about teamwork while doing the job. This isn't the most efficient way to learn it, but it is often the only way we do. In my program where new employees spend two weeks in orientation training, they graduate and go to their separate treatment units, and hope they can readily assimilate into the team.

This is sometimes just a shot in the dark. Each person must find a way to adapt to the new team environment. We hold quarterly team meetings, but these aren't enough to solidify the **Teamwork and Communication** vital to producing quality care.

When people work together for a long period of time without any turnover, the foundation of a real team takes shape. Then turnover, like cancer, eats away at the team's soul.

Before the supervisors realize it, they're back in basic team building mode. Let me say right here, there isn't anything right or wrong with this process. It just is. We would like to spend more time building a team, but it is not cost effective. We have youth to take care of and they don't leave at 4 PM and go home. It takes time to build solid teams and practice effective communication. Some supervisors act like real coaches and spend a lot of time developing their respective teams. Others do not. They aren't blessed with the foresight or insight necessary to accomplish this task. We can teach the supervisors what they need to do, but they still must want to do it. Coaching requires that supervisors want to build a team that can function without their direct guidance and support. They must believe in the Y Theory of management: that all people come to work to do their very best. It is the coach's role to nurture this in each individual on the team.

The truth is that many people don't want to coach a team. They want to supervise it. Coaching takes extra effort. For most supervisors, control is the issue. They don't fully understand or appreciate the power of the team gestalt. For the rest, it's just they don't know how to do it. There is a significant difference between the two activities. Supervisors tell the team what to do, monitor its performance, intervene when necessary to get it back on track and remain somewhat aloof and above the process.

The coaching supervisor realizes how important the principle of **Teamwork and Communication** is and makes every effort to teach it to his team. This requires an unselfish attitude, a lot of physical and mental energy and a true commitment to making the team function as a unit and not like a disparate gathering of clinical prima donnas.

When there is a shared effort and a common vision, quality work gets done. This is readily seen in the units that are supervised by people with a coaching and mentoring focus. True, work gets done in both types of settings. It's just that in the collegial environment, where all team members are pulling together, the team produces more, with less effort and greater joy. There is nothing in a clinical program more exciting to watch than a well-disciplined team working with a difficult client. This teamwork takes time to foster in a group of individuals who come to the work place with different ethnic, religious, family, work and education backgrounds. When it happens most of us who see the beauty in their collective genius providing quality care would love to clone it and spread it around. Sad to say, this is not one organism that can be cloned.

What does it take to build a team and get it to effectively communicate? Let me share some of the most basic steps with you.

1.   **First, there must be a commitment on the part of the supervisor to be a coach.** He must desire to be the team leader, the mentor, role model for the members that it takes to be a team. He must accept that he will be teaching more than supervising. Rather than directing someone to do something, he will be showing the team member how to do it.

2.   **Second, the individual members of the unit must want to commit to being a team**. If all do, the effort is much easier. If there are people on the team holding out, then the building takes a whole lot longer.

3.   Third, time must be spent on team building. There is no way to do it while the services are being provided. This is application of team, not team building. Some activities can foster a team effort and if processed well, lead the team forward toward a greater sense of the whole. However, as one of our program's vice presidents once said, "Building a team in a residential treatment setting is like trying to change a flat tire on a moving vehicle." It can be done, but it isn't easy, and certainly not pretty.

4.   Fourth, the coach and the team members need to set goals for the team. We write individual service plans for clients. What is needed is a team development plan with goals, action steps, time frames in which to complete the steps, and measurement tools to let us know if the steps are successfully completed. This plan needs to be reviewed monthly for the first year, quarterly for the second year and then biannually after that. In this way, all can keep track of the progress being made. This monitoring further fosters the team's development.

5.   Fifth, the team must be open to feedback from internal and external consultants. When outside observers observe the team in action and provide it with ways to improve its performance, the team can grow. This really requires that egos be suppressed. There is no other way to objectively receive feedback. This applies to the supervisor as well as the individual team members. If we define feedback as information given freely to us so that we can learn and grow, then it will be much easier to accept it.

6.   Sixth, the team needs to study how other successful teams function. The team needs to read and learn from other sources and share this with one another. It is true that all teams are unique, but there are some common threads that run through all team effort. Understanding these from a pragmatic perspective raises the knowledge base of the entire team.

7.   **Finally, the team must practice communicating with one another in all media**: the spoken word, written word, and most importantly non-verbal or body language cues that foster the sense that all are "on the same page." This takes time and patience, but once it is mastered, the team can then be functioning at optimum levels and the outcome is that the people served receive the highest quality of care.

I haven't specifically addressed the second part of **Teamwork and Communication**. We can be working together, pulling in the same way that the members of a sculling team do, but unless we are communicating with one another some of our efforts will be lost in the process. The seventh step listed above is the most difficult one for most teams to master. The reasons are many. The fact remains that unless we openly and consistently communicate with one another the greater team effort is minimized.

Every human being possesses some ability to communicate with others. Some are more verbally gifted. Others can write exceptionally well, but yet can't verbally communicate in the same facile manner. Then there are those who are masters of the non-verbal communication process. As part of team building, there is a need to practice the communication process as well. Protocols need to be set in place to insure that written communication takes place. Each team member must be encouraged to practice both verbal and written skills. As coach and mentor, the supervisor needs to model both skills and use every opportunity to teach these to the team members.

Team meetings need to occur every day, and more often, when there is a call to develop strategies to meet the program's immediate needs. One way that residential programs facilitate this is to have shift meetings before the work is undertaken.

This helps everyone understand what the clinical plan is for the next shift. Stopping what we are doing and planning with the team members present fosters good communication. Unless this meeting takes place, there is more than likely going to be some breakdown later in the shift. This is the FRAM (motor oil filter commercial) concept at work again. "Pay now or pay later."

Another way to promote effective communication is to use a communication log. It is one way to get on the same page. Each team member writes what he or she did during the shift, sharing strategies, concerns and any other information that can promote the total team effort. Other team members read and initial the log when they are done. This way, each person can effectively say, "I am on the same page."

The use of email is the latest wrinkle in the communication process. It helps all of us transcend time and space. It can be broadcast to a wider audience because it is not bound by time. It is easy, fast, can be saved, printed and stored as archives. The one drawback is that the technology must be available at all times, working seamlessly, and most importantly, team members must want to use it. Unless they are committed to doing so, there will be a communication breakdown.

There is nothing that works better for building a team and fostering communication than the weekly face-to-face meeting of the team members. An agenda for the meeting is essential to insure time is managed effectively. But there needs to be a portion of every meeting where new ideas are shared, new business is discussed and the team members have an equal opportunity to state in what direction they believe the team effort should take.

These meetings are not easy to schedule, and yet they are essential if the team is to fully develop. Depending on the nature of the program, the leaders need to figure out a way to make them happen. Unless the team meets regularly, there is no way that the principle of **Teamwork and Communication** can be effectively implemented.

It's exciting to watch a team come together and provide quality services to the people it serves. Team members share in something greater than themselves when the team is functioning well. This helps to reinforce the value and importance of **Teamwork and Communication** as a guiding principle for the program.

Up to this point, I've focused on the caregivers as team members. I haven't said anything about those receiving the care and how they fit into the team effort. It is essential to include them in the process as well. True, we are the primary source of the service we are providing. We are trained to be human service professionals. We get paid to provide the services we are contracted for and we need to do this without any assistance on the part of the people we serve. Yet, when we include them in the process, they are likely to respond more favorably to the actions we are taking. When people feel a part of something, they tend to participate more fully. So how do we do this?

First, we include people in developing their own individual training plans. Whether we are teachers, counselors, doctors and nurses, mental health case workers or day care specialists, when we include the people in planning how to address any physical, mental or emotional need, they will respond more favorably. The question is, who is this for? Their answer will simply be, for me. Given this acknowledgement, we can begin to work together on addressing the needs.

This doesn't mean that we do the work for them. No, it is a collaborative effort. In fact, they will ultimately do most of the work. We are their guides and supports. We've been invited into their lives and, therefore, must make the best of the invitation. It must be to provide the highest quality of care we are capable of giving whatever limitations we have.

Second, we need to ask the clients for their input on a range of things. For instance we may want to know how we are doing, and what can we do to improve the quality of service. We need to ask them. Their input is essential if we are to be effective. They are the recipients of what we do. If they are of sound mind and judgment, they can be our most important source of feedback. All we need to do is be open to listening. Most of what they tell us will be valuable, but not always applicable or feasible. When they realize that we really listened to them and implemented what they suggested, they will be more apt to partner with us in the future. In so doing, we provide better services. When they experience a change in the program that enhances their growth and development, they will be even more engaged.

Third, we must realize we can't do it alone. We as a team can't make all the calls and expect that they will produce quality care. The feedback loop is necessary if we are to become a model program that lives its mission, philosophy and principles. The collegial effort is exhilarating. As clients develop and grow, the team is energized. As the team is energized, the clients are excited about the healthy, happy environment in which they are living. One success feeds the next one. It is synergistic. It is the magic of the human service relationship. After a while, it's hard to tell who is helping whom.

Fourth, there is nothing more dispiriting than to think and feel that a person has no control over his or her life. This leads first to depression, and secondly, feeds the cancer of low self-esteem. When a person is engaged in the design, implementation and management of a program, he will develop and grow more quickly and accept more responsibility for the outcome of the service being provided. The more a person contributes to the overall plan of the team effort, the greater will be the team's success.

Finally, a team is made up of all the players. If we, as service providers, proceed with the notion that we are omniscient and omnipotent, we will turn off the real power in any program and that is the power of a person to control his own destiny. We must begin to truly believe that even a hardened criminal is ultimately responsible for the outcome of his life, and will make the necessary changes so that he can one day return to the community and be a productive member of society. There may be some that are beyond salvation, but that is not the issue in this discussion. We can always believe the best for all people. Whether or not they achieve what they set out to do and realize their own human potential is in their control. We must engage them in taking that path and nudge them along the way when they lose motivation or focus. Reflecting back to the principle stated earlier, "We alone can do it but we can't do it alone."

How can we implement this principle unless we are consistently using all the principles previously discussed? The answer is simply. We can't. **Teamwork and Communication** requires that we teach by example. It demands that we hold our clients responsible for their behavior. To be an effective program, we must provide a high degree of structure and clear expectations for change.

Most of all, it requires that we are with the people we serve and are meaningfully interacting with them. All the principles are intertwined. Leave one out and the others are less effective and the program suffers. Combine them and the outcomes produced are sometimes beyond our own vision. This is what makes the human services profession such an exciting, rewarding, energizing way to spend one's life: providing quality care to those in need.

In conclusion, **Teamwork and Communication** can and will drive our programs toward the highest quality care we can provide. Let me end this chapter with another parable.

The Parable of the Stone Soup

A woman wanted to make a pot of soup but she didn't have any vegetables. She got a large stone and placed it into a pot of boiling water. She needed some vegetables so she went to the neighbor next door and told her that she was making a pot of stone soup, but needed some carrots to give it flavor. She made her a deal. If she would give her some carrots, she would save her a bowl of the stone soup. She was only too happy to offer her some carrots because she wanted to taste stone soup.

The woman went around the block to each one of her neighbors and gathered as many different kinds of vegetables as she could and made each of her neighbors the same deal. They gave her onions, potatoes, green peppers, celery, pinto beans, and more.

When the soup was finished, the woman called all her neighbors to her house to taste the stone soup. They all declared that this was the best soup they had ever eaten.

They enjoyed it so much that all of them asked for the recipe. She told them it was very simple. Find a large, smooth stone and clean it well. Put it in a pot of boiling water. Then find yourself some good neighbors who have a lot of vegetables.

We can take any program and make it into one that provides quality services, if we have the raw materials and work together. The formula is that simple.

POSITIVE ROLE MODELING

"Teaching people by setting an example"

Positive Role Modeling is teaching people by setting an example.

This principle is the one that is most dependent upon the individual team members of a program. As a whole, the program can be a positive model if the people who work in it are positive role models. True, the program isn't a person. It is made up of many different persons. Each one is charged with being a positive role model. Each one must fully comprehend that what each says or does will be taught to the people being served by the program. When caregivers function as positive role models, the program will be providing quality care.

This is the easiest principle to understand, but the most difficult to fix if it is out of kilter. How do we go about teaching an entire system that whatever is being said or done at any give time affects the entire system? Let me give you an example from the residential placement setting.

A team member is addressing a youth's behavior. He is doing his best to provide quality care. He fully understands the principles and attempts to demonstrate them in his day to day job related responsibilities. As he is intervening with the youth, he does something that is disrespectful to him. He calls him a "dingbat" for not working harder in school and taking his education seriously. Out of fear of reprisal, the youth takes the intervention but thinks, "They tell us not to call each other names, but he's calling me a dingbat." The intervention is over, but the youth is not fully sure the team member cares about him because he called him a name. Later on, the same youth calls another youth the same name and is addressed for being disrespectful. He wants to shout out and tell everybody, "Hey, you do it, why can't I?"

Now let me ask you the question again. How do you fix a program when the team members aren't being positive role models? It's not easy because just one small interaction like the one described above sows seeds of discontent in a youth.

For any program to be successful and provide the highest quality of care, it is essential that professional expectations be taught to all employees, family members and people with any kind of vested interest in seeing it succeed. Once these expectations are made clear, it is much easier for individuals to be positive role models.

Some might argue that being a positive role model is self-explanatory. In some ways, it is. It is also difficult sometimes for a person to see just how one mistake can affect the whole system.

Let's look at this issue in a global way. How many of you know a lawyer joke? Okay, so you know more than one. These jokes are about whom? They poke fun at lawyers and if they were all true, no one would ever want a lawyer to be representing him. Lawyers, like other human beings, aren't perfect. If one lawyer makes a mistake, the rest of the profession becomes the butt of jokes the world over. Is it fair? No, indeed not. It is, to use a legal term, prejudicial. Does it happen? Yes, all the time. Next to politicians, lawyers are the most despised group of people in the country, so the polls say. But we all know at least one lawyer that we trust, can consult with and respect and admire. Sure, it's our own lawyer. If we didn't trust and respect him, we would not retain his services.

Programs, like lawyers, are often subjected to injustices and treated unfairly because one of the employees makes a serious mistake.

Here is another example. Just because a father is an alcoholic and gets arrested time and time again, this doesn't mean that the rest of the family members are alcoholics and support his irresponsible behavior. More than likely, they are embarrassed and wish he would go into treatment and live a sober life. They might do everything within their power to get him to change, but unless he is willing to do so, they can do nothing. Yet, they are all subject to judgment because of his behavior.

One doctor or nurse makes a mistake. Yes, it's a serious one. He prescribed the wrong medication, the nurse dispensed it and the patient dies from an adverse reaction. Now the entire hospital staff comes under close scrutiny because of the error in judgment. Even though there was no malicious intent to harm the client, the situation causes major public relations and legal problems for the hospital.

A school has a great reputation for academic excellence. It has a faculty that is superior to most. There are many masters-level educators and some doctors on the team. There is one teacher who is loved and respected by all the students. Sometime during the school year, it is discovered that this highly respected individual is having an affair with a married woman on the faculty. Everyone finds out. The students, parents and the community are devastated by the news. The school's reputation is tainted by the behavior of one of its most respected members.

In a large city, the police force works diligently to "protect and serve" the public. One cop is busted for being corrupt. Now, everyone on the force is faced with a tarnished image because of the behavior of the one individual who failed to live up to the mission and principles that all police officers are required to follow.

I can give you example after example of how positive role modeling is essential if a program, a hospital, a family, a school, or a police force is to provide quality care. It is tragic that one person's not being a positive role model can affect the entire system. As I stated earlier, this is what makes it so difficult to fix. When one member does something, it affects all the other members of the program. One father, one cop or one teacher can sow bad seeds that take years to uproot.

As you read this you might be saying, "It isn't fair that all should suffer for the failure of one." I agree, but that isn't the way life is. All of us at some time in our lives suffered because of the behavior of one individual who was a part of our program but failed to be a positive role model.

Positive Role Modeling is the principle that is most dependent upon each individual's performance. This may not be fair and we may not like it, but it is a fact of life. A program is only as strong as its weakest link and this generally is the team member who fails in some situation to be a positive role model.

Some of you might be squirming in your seats right now. Your eyeballs are restless. Am I implying that we have to be perfect human beings? No, indeed not, because that would be impossible. What this principle implies is this: We must aspire to be as positive a role model as is humanly possible. There is no way we can be perfect human beings. There aren't any. But can we expect that a member of our program strives to be a positive role model at all times? We can. Will some fall short of this? Yes, they will. When it does, we'll deal with the fallout and move on. Just like I'm not going to indict the Los Angeles Police Department as a whole for the Rodney King Affair, I'm not going to judge an entire program for the poor choices made by a few individuals.

What does it take to be a positive role model? It takes making a commitment to the mission of the program whatever the mission might be. It requires a lot of hard work on the part of each team member. It requires that each team member in the program commits to fulfilling the mission and being open to feedback from supervisors and peers when there is evidence he is not demonstrating positive role modeling. It's tough to live by such high standards. If we don't, we can't expect to provide quality care.

There is a principle that I'd like to share with you that fits right here: ***The whole is not only made up of all the separate parts, but how those parts interact with one another.***

If one person is functioning outside the boundaries, the entire system suffers. Unless each person accepts how important his part is, it will be difficult for the system to function as a positive role model to the people it serves. This is a tall order. No one would deny this. Still, it is essential that the highest standards are set or quality service will suffer.

Until now, I've focused upon how a program is affected when the members aren't being positive role models. This is a natural tendency for all of us who want to provide the highest quality care. We tend to focus on the problem and not the solution.

What is the solution?

First, every member of every program must be constantly reminded how important positive role modeling is. From the director to the newest employee, all need to embrace this principle. Fathers must realize that their children will learn more by what they do, not what they say. Counselors can preach responsible living, but if they fail to meet with a client at the time scheduled, the client will question their integrity and their sincerity. A hospital may advertise its "state of the art" laser surgery procedures, but when the rooms are not cleaned well and the nurses are rude and indifferent to the patient, the quality of care will be questioned.

Whenever there is some behavior that contradicts the mission statement, the program will be adversely affected. It is important for all who have a vested interest in the success of any program, system or family to be positive role models for it, in it and most significantly, outside of it. We may want to deny it, but we are a reflection of our work. We are representatives of the programs we work for even when we're not on the clock. This is a hard pill to swallow, but it is a simple truism.

One of the strangest experiences I ever had was attending a statewide Drug and Alcohol Programs Conference. I won't name the state so that I don't embarrass anyone. At the conference, people were supposed to be sharing information about their programs, learning new ways to treat the chemically addicted, and in general, improve the quality of services being offered to the clients their programs served. What I discovered was the conference was one long party. Nearly every room was hosting a party. There was booze flowing and I heard that many folks were "recreationally using marijuana". I was appalled and left the conference early thinking about what hypocrites these people were.

Drinking is legal but using marijuana isn't in most states. Even so, when people in the recovery field behave in this way, it's just a matter of time before the clients they serve will discover what is really happening. Our clients are very sensitive to who we are, what we are about and can read us like a book. When we are preaching one thing and doing something else, then we're going to be labeled hypocrites. They may not tell us this to our faces. What they will do is listen to what we say and think, "That's not what they do." So the service we are providing is negated because our clients don't see us as positive role models.

How can we insure that we are being positive role models?

Second, we need to make our expectations clear for everyone. Does this language sound familiar? This is **Program Integrity** fusing with positive role modeling. By expecting all of us to be positive role models, we are setting the stage for it to happen. There is an old therapeutic principle that I was taught more than a quarter century ago that fits here quite nicely. It is: *If you're going to talk the talk, we need to walk the walk*. When we talk about being positive role models, we challenge ourselves to act upon what we say. All we need to do is have one client, one family member or patient say to us, "You're a hypocrite!" and we'll feel the pressure to be a better role model. Being in the human service profession is difficult. Sometimes it feels like we're between a rock and a hard place. We want our clients to get well, stop drinking, develop their human potential, and yet we, the change agents may need to do some of the same work ourselves. Who was it that said, "Heal thyself?" The statement applies. Working on becoming a positive role model is the first step toward healing.

When training new counselors, one of the cautions I have for them is to never discuss with their clients issues that are unfinished in their own lives. This is what I tell them: "Since you haven't put closure to it in your own life, you may inadvertently work out your issue with your client and not truly serve him. Your role is not to do your counseling through them. Your role is to guide and support them in the healing process."

Third, we need to practice being positive role models. This means we work at it just like we expect our family members, clients, patients or students to work on their stuff. We may need to post this principle on the wall in front of our desks to constantly remind us what we are supposed to be and do.

This may sound silly, but it is one of the primary strategies taught in the reframing process that is a part of Neuro-linguistic Programming. If you want to change something, surround yourself with sights, sounds and things that evoke the image of what you want to change. *Successories* has made a great business out of this concept. It has lovely photographs of the natural world with inspirational phrases printed above, below or on them to get us to associate the image with the principle it is promoting. For example, an eight person rowing team is shown working together. It's an enchanting image and the phrase placed along with it is *Teamwork: Everyone pulling in the same direction*. The image for positive role modeling might be a father walking with his son, hand-in-hand, and the son, holding on to his little brother and walking along hand-in-hand. Of course, the phrase would be: *Teaching by setting an example*. Whatever way we can remind ourselves to be positive role models we need to do it.

Fourth, we need to encourage the 360-degree feedback loop. We all need to give each other feedback as we move closer and closer to that impossible state called perfection. If we want our people to be positive role models, we all need to commit to giving each other feedback. It's not enough to get feedback from just our supervisor. We need to get it from all of the people with whom we work and even those we serve. When this 360 feedback loop is in place, the movement toward being a positive role model is greatly enhanced. There is little doubt that when we are being observed and supported and prompted by more than one person, the rate of change becomes nearly exponential. Feedback is feedback. It is information given to someone to help people grow.

Fifth, we need to reward positive role modeling when it is practical and cost efficient to do so. Positive reinforcement of positive role modeling sounds like it might create a doubling effect. When we see someone being a positive role model, we reward him in some way. He is encouraged by our gesture and works harder to role model even more. We see his efforts and we are inspired to do the same to support his renewed effort. In some ways, it's almost like a healthy contagion. Success breeds more success. Happiness promotes the desire for more happiness. Positive role modeling causes us to want to be a more positive role model. When a program is defined by how it models the behaviors, attitudes and beliefs it wants the people it serves to learn, there is no limit to what it can achieve.

Sixth, positive role modeling is at the core of what we do. If we don't believe that the service we are providing, the knowledge we are teaching, the care we are giving is the best we can give, then we will fall far short of our goal. We must believe that the majority of us will do whatever it takes to achieve this goal. We don't enter this profession to fail. There is enough failure on the part of our clients, students, patients or inmates to make up for a lifetime of losing. Sometimes we fail ourselves to realize that it is totally within our control to be the most positive role models we can be. When we are, we give those we serve something so see, hear, feel and to model.

As you are reading this chapter, did you happen to notice how this principle dovetails into the previous ones? We can be positive role models only when we are with our people and meaningfully interacting with them.

We can achieve our goals by maintaining program integrity. The expectations and structure are created, implemented and modeled by us. When we teach our people ARE, we do so by modeling it in our own lives first, and then within the structure of the program. When something isn't working, we own the problem, assess what needs to be fixed and then fix it. All these steps are the basis for positive role modeling. We model what we want our people to learn and then celebrate once they have mastered the lesson.

There is nothing magical about this process. It's as ancient as the pyramids. It's as simple as adding one plus one. Sometimes though, it's easier to pass over the razor's edge than it is to be a consistent positive role model. We all have our boogies and bad breath. We all have moods and sometimes dwell in them. We all are given to sloughs of despond. We rage when we're mistreated and rejoice when we experience a financial or emotional windfall achieved often through no concerted effort on our parts. If we believe in the essence of the principle that we are to be positive role models for the people in our programs, we will slide right on over that razor's edge without getting a nick and smile as if we do this all the time.

The program for which I work adopted the symbol of Sisyphus for its logo. If you recall, Sisyphus offended the gods and was condemned to roll a rock up a hill every day of his life. At the end of the day, when he'd achieved his goal and would have liked to rest, the rock would tumble back down to the bottom. The next day, he would have to start all over again.

Viewed from a practical point of view, this would be the consummate image of how depressing life can be: a daily struggle that repeats itself day after day until we die. We view it from the perspective promoted by Albert Camus, the existential philosopher.

At the end of his essay entitled, "The Myth of Sisyphus", he wrote, "…we can only imagine Sisyphus happy." This is what positive role modeling means to us. We don't see life's struggle as meaningless or hopeless. We accept it and model happiness in our work, and most of all, in our personal lives

Let me conclude this chapter with a parable.

The Parable of the Mower Man

There was a man who loved to mow the lawn. He took great pride in the way his lawn looked after he cut it. He cut it with the grain using a reel mower so that when he was done, it looked like a manicured fairway on an exclusive country club. His neighbors wondered what made him spend so much time cutting the lawn. They got on their riding mowers and whacked away once a week and got the job done. They couldn't be bothered spending a lot of time cutting grass when there were so many other things to do with their spare time. Now, when the man got too old to cut the grass with his trusty reel lawn mower, he asked his son if he would mind cutting it for him. His son was a busy man, but he knew that his father loved the way the lawn looked when it was cut with the reel mower so he said, "Yes, I will father." The son continued to cut the lawn for his father until the old man passed away one day while sitting in his lawn chair admiring his beautiful lawn. After the funeral, the mother told the son that she was going to get someone else to cut the lawn for her so that he didn't have to do it any more. He told her, "Mom, I don't mind. Dad taught me well."

We learn by doing. We teach by modeling. We provide quality care when we are teaching by positive modeling what we want our people to learn.

DIGNITY & RESPECT

"Showing care and concern for all peoples' needs"

Dignity and Respect is showing care and concern for all people's needs.
There is nothing we won't do to meet the needs of our clients. We break down barriers to make sure that there isn't anything a client needs while he is in our care. We do everything in our power to insure that our people succeed.

What is **Care and Concern**? It is simply reaching out to people in any way we can so they think and feel they are receiving the highest quality care we can give. We don't tell them we care about them. By our actions, we show them. In nursing homes, we bathe them when necessary. We stay after school to tutor a student who is having a hard time with his math. As doctors, we sit down with our patient and explain in lay person's terms what his medical condition is and suggest treatment options and listen to what the patient has to say. Whatever it takes to meet the needs, we do.

Depending upon our work environment, the needs can vary greatly. Our ability to meet them is what defines us as professionals. Anyone can sustain qualitative and quantitative effort for a short period of time. What separates us from being amateurs at the work that we do is more than we get paid to do it. We possess the ability to work through all the barriers, boundaries, set backs, and still meet our people's needs. We don't ask them if they want their needs to be met. We meet them because this is our responsibility. We accept this and move toward achieving this outcome with joy and vigor. Anything less would be unprofessional.

Care is not something that can be talked about; it must be shown. We can express concern. But "care" is a verb. It is not a noun. Some might want it to be in certain contexts. Generally, it is the action we take to meet people's needs. Care is the quintessential activity of our profession. It doesn't matter what milieu in which we work, if we can't demonstrate care for our people, then we are not going to provide quality services. CARE is so important that CARE is part of the title of this book!

So how does "Care" form the foundation for this principle, **Dignity and Respect**? Unless we can truly demonstrate care for our people, there is no way we can treat them with dignity and respect. All humans have a right to be treated with dignity. They don't need to earn our respect. We just give it to them. Whether or not they reciprocate is up to them. We do not need to be respected nor do we demand it. For those new to this profession, the struggle is to find out how we get past the resistance many of our youth demonstrate when it comes to changing their lives? One way to resolve this issue is to understand the principles of resistance.

Principles of Resistance

The first principle is *"There is resistance to change in individuals and groups."*

Change takes work. However, people don't resist change; people resist being changed. It requires the person to overcome the human inertia of status quo and move toward a new way to be.

This can be frightening for some, energy draining for others and unwanted by a select few. The implications of this principle for our work are far reaching. For those people who have little energy with which to use in the change process, we must be the catalysts for them. In performing this action, we are bound to lose a little bit of our own energy. We often become the catalyst for them. If they are frightened by what they are going through, then we need to become the voice of peace and tranquility. We need to intervene and assure them that once the initial fear is gone, the outcome will be worth the momentary terror. For those who just plain don't want to change, we need to be persuasive, build their trust, and encourage them to consider how the change will eventually make a difference in the quality of their lives. This requires patience on our part because they are not going to undertake this path willingly. Only when they see the value in what they can ultimately achieve will they move away from resistance and begin to work on changing their lives. Once they realize there is a benefit to making the change, they will do it with joy and enthusiasm.

The second principle of resistance **is "We cannot eliminate the resistance immediately."**

What happens when we try to do this? There is more resistance. People don't like to be forced to change. When we make something mandatory, hackles rise and the resistance we feel is almost palpable. By understanding this principle, we can plan strategies that will help the person begin to make the changes at his own pace. Most importantly, we will not become impatient and make demands. We will consider how to challenge the person to undertake the change process. We might have to function for a while as a catalyst or change agent. Once the person embraces the need for the change in his or her life, we can step back and just watch as it takes place.

The third principle is *"We acknowledge that it exists."* When we sense that a person is being resistant, we can simply say, "I'm sensing some resistance right now from you. What is the resistance about?" Notice that I'm asking the question as if the resistance has a life of its own. I'm not asking the person to tell me about him. I'm asking the person to tell me about the resistance, the force that is keeping him from moving forward. In so doing, I'm guiding the person away from being resistant, first by understanding it, and then, by committing to doing something to get over it. This is not an attack. I'm not going after the person for being resistant. I'm challenging him to describe it and do something about it. In this interaction, I'm insuring that the person's dignity is maintained. He may not want to be resistant. He may not even know that he is being resistant. It is possible, we know, for some of us to be in denial about something and not even know it. This is the very essence of the denial process. So acknowledging the resistance is part of breaking down the denial. There is nothing magical in breaking through the denial. It requires some inquiry. It demands that we listen carefully for the responses and not judge the person too harshly if he says or does something that isn't what we want to hear.

The fourth principle of resistance is *"We begin to work with the resistance and over time it diffuses."*

Imagine for a moment what it must be like for a person who is told by his doctor to lose a significant amount of weight or his life will be drastically shortened. What do you suppose the patient will do? He probably will be resistant to the change. He spent his life gaining the weight. He may even be proud of the paunch he has grown.

Now he must do something about it or dire consequences will result. For a period of time, he may experience some depression. He knows that what the doctor says is true. Slowly, he begins to commit to the change, and over a period of time, his resistance diffuses. He begins to lose weight. He feels much better. He can bend over without struggling. He can walk up the steps without huffing and puffing. His knees don't ache because he's carrying a whole lot less weight around with him. Over a period of time, there is a magical transformation.

The once, heavy man looks in the mirror and sees the shape of the young man he once was. His self-esteem returns. He asks himself, "How did I ever let myself go that way?" He vows to make the weight loss program successful. When he goes in for his first visit after the consultation, the doctor is amazed to see how much weight he has lost. The man is proud and tells the doctor, "You haven't seen anything yet." A year later, the weight is still coming off slowly but surely. He continues to work on his health and well being. What has happened is a total transformation that was initially met with a lot of resistance. As you can see, once the person commits to the change, we need to do little more than to support its continuation.

This is what makes the human service profession so exciting. When people change and grow and we've played some small part in the process, we get to share vicariously in their success. It is theirs, but we've had a gentle hand in it. When we treat our people with **Dignity and Respect**, this is the kind of outcome we can expect.

By understanding the *Principles of Resistance*, we can work with resistant clients and still treat them with utmost **Dignity and Respect**.

Earlier in this chapter I commented on the need for expressing concern as well. Concern is something we can talk about with our people. It is a simple statement like this, "I am concerned about you." When we say this to a person, it means that we are aware of something in him that may need attention. In the case of the man, it was his obesity. Concern is as diverse as the individual needs of people. By expressing concern, we are engaging the person in dialogue. We aren't saying, "Hey, there's something wrong with you. You've got a problem." We're expressing our concern. The person may not even be aware of what we're pointing out to him. The concern is like feedback. It can be accepted or rejected. As long as it is given and taken in this context, it will not be seen as judgment. Now, if we were to say, "Hey, I am concerned about you. You need to do something about your behavior."

This statement of concern is passing into judgment. True, all statements of concern possess some element of judgment. We see or hear something and we may determine the person to whom we are expressing our concern may want to know what we are thinking or feeling. But true concern stops there. Judgment makes the person feel like there is something wrong with him if he doesn't jump up and say, "Hallelujah, I've got a problem. Now what do I do?" We will always walk a fine line between concern and judgment. So be it. Realizing the nature of this concept can guide us to make effective interventions that consistently support a person's dignity and respect.

How many times have you been affected by someone's feedback about your performance? Think about how it feels when someone passes judgment on what you've done or said. If you respect the person and they tell you with respect, it's much easier to sit and listen to his feedback.

When it is not done this way, how many of us just blow off what is being said? I know I do, even if what is being said may in the end benefit me. It's human nature to want to be treated with dignity and respect. Since we work in the human service profession, it seems only natural and proper to treat our people with the same amount of dignity and respect we want ourselves.

Many colleagues who hear me teaching this say that I am really teaching the Golden Rule: *"Treat others as you would have them treat you."* Yes, it is the Golden Rule with the additional caveat that we are responsible for providing for the needs of others. They are not responsible for taking care of us. We strive to treat them with dignity and respect because it is the right thing to do. We may not get the same treatment from them. This is when we apply the principles of resistance and realize their attack on us may be just their resistance rising up and spewing out of their mouths. Given that understanding, we can be patient and continue to work toward their embracing change in their lives at their own pace.

What do you do when change is absolutely necessary and there is little time in which to get the person to change? Hey, isn't that the universal condition of the work we do? How many of you wouldn't like more time, money and opportunity to do more for the people you serve? This is one constant we face in human service. We never seem to have enough time, money, other resources or human energy to do the work we do.

So what do we do? We do the best we can to provide quality care regardless of the barriers that we face. What more can I say about this. Neither you nor I can spontaneously add money to the program's coffers. We can't grant more time for treatment when the client's insurance company says, "No more."

We can't extend the school year because one student doesn't fully comprehend geometry. We can't, tragically, extend an inmate's stay in prison when we know that he has not internalized any of the principles we have tried to teach him. Life is full of these inconsistencies. We can only strive to apply these principles, do our best to provide the highest quality care we can and pray that our efforts will take root and grow in the body, mind and spirit of the person we've committed our lives to helping.

You may notice I've spent a lot of time on describing each word in this principle, **Dignity and Respect**. It is important that we clearly understand each word so the principle will come to life for us as we apply it. I didn't focus much on the "wants" of our people. What people want is not within our sphere of responsibility. An inmate may want to get out, have sex, drink or read pornography, but we aren't going to provide any of this for him. These are wants. These are things that he lost as a result of his criminality. What he needs is to become a responsible person. We will teach this every chance that we can.

A student may want to go home and not do any homework. He'd rather play Nintendo instead of practicing his math times-tables. We assign homework to him so he can learn his time tables now rather than when he grows up and feels some embarrassment because he can't multiply 6 times 7 and get 42.

A resident may want to go on a home pass so he can see his girlfriend, family and friends. He's not ready to go, but he really wants to leave. He is bent out of shape when his pass request is turned down. We tell him that he needs to learn to separate "wants" from "needs."

He is not yet ready to go home, because, thus far in treatment, he hasn't demonstrated the commitment to self-control and sober-living we believe is essential before we permit him to go home for a weekend. He gets feedback about what he needs to do and encouragement to continue to be a responsible person.

In the nursing home, an elderly lady wants to go outside and sit in the sun. The aides tell her she can't go outside because the sun is too hot for her. She has skin cancer and is under doctor's order not to be outside for any reason. But she wants to go out. She doesn't care what the doctor says. She wants to sit in the sun and feel the warm glow. The aides don't take her out.

In each of the above situations, the people we serve are attempting to fulfill their wants, not their needs.

One of the most difficult tasks we face in human service or in our families is to guide people toward meeting their needs and postponing some of their wants. There are so many wants that we sometimes are overwhelmed with the demands placed upon us. It is essential that we focus on needs. At all times, we need to treat our people with dignity and respect. It is hard to tell an elderly woman she can't go and sit in the sun. Who among us wants to be told we can't go outside and get warm?

What we must do, at all times, is what is in the best interest of our people. This is not always a popular position to take, but then again, being in the human service profession is not about being popular with our people. It means providing a service to them and sometimes this causes them discomfort. We don't do this just to make their lives miserable. We do it because it is, as I said a moment ago, in their best interest.

Separating wants from needs is possibly the most difficult thing for most human beings to do. We need so few things, yet we are constantly in a state of flux when we aren't satisfying our wants. We might even describe our wants as needs. I need to eat. I need a new car. I need a new shotgun. I need to go for a walk. I need this or that. Most of the time, what we are stating is a want. As human services professionals, we need to understand the difference. Our work becomes much easier when we focus purely on need and leave the satisfying of the want to our client once he is no longer in our care. This doesn't mean we are insensitive to people's wants. Life would be boring if we spent our existence fulfilling our needs and nothing else. This would be bare existence, survival, and nothing more. No, living a happy life is something we certainly hope each client achieves. This is where needs and wants blur together. When we are providing care and concern, it is our task to guide and support people in understanding the difference between these two things. First, they must achieve their needs, and then address those wants that are in their best interest.

When we truly believe in and apply the principle of **Dignity and Respect**, our people receive the highest quality of care. It doesn't matter what they've done, what they've said, what their transgressions against society are, if we are to be professionals, we'll treat them with **Dignity and Respect**.

Let me share a parable with you.

The Parable of the Kazoo Player

There once was a child who was proud of his ability to play the kazoo. He mastered the instrument when he was only four years old. Every waking moment, he played his kazoo. When he was playing, he was at peace with himself.

But when he turned 6, he was told he'd have to go to school. Now, he didn't mind going at first, because he could play his kazoo as he walked to and from school. It troubled him that during school he wasn't permitted to play. This meant he wasn't able to practice for more than six hours of his day. He didn't like this. One day, he had enough. He pulled out his kazoo and started playing in class. He played so softly that his teacher didn't hear him. His classmates did and they began to smile and pay attention to him rather than to the teacher. She finally realized what was going on and walked back to where the boy was playing and told him to stop. He did, for awhile, but when he was feeling the urge to play again, he pulled out his kazoo and continued making music.

This pattern was repeated three times before the teacher finally demanded he give her the kazoo. He reluctantly gave it to her. At the end of the day, she gave it back, but instructed him to leave it at home. She wrote a note for him to take home to his mother and father describing what happened. He never gave it to them. He didn't leave his kazoo at home. He carried it with him wherever he went, even to school. His playing continued. He wouldn't stop. The teacher made him stop over and over again. Whenever he could get away with it, he'd play. Eventually, he was sent to the principal's office. His parents had to come to school for a conference, and the whole situation came to a head.

His parents told him that he'd have to stop bringing the kazoo to school. He told them that the kazoo was his life. He wanted to be a kazoo player and nothing would stop him from achieving his goal. They took his kazoo, but he managed to get another one. They took that one too, but he kept getting more of them. He hid them everywhere and so they couldn't keep him from getting his hands on a kazoo and playing.

Since he wouldn't leave his kazoo at home when he went to school, the principal told the parents he couldn't return. The parents were at their wit's end with their son and told him so. He just continued to tell them that all he wanted to do was be a kazoo player. They couldn't understand him. They sent him to counseling. When the counselor told the parents to let the kid play his kazoo, they labeled the counselor a "communist" and pulled him from treatment. The boy realized there wasn't going to be any peace and so, one day, he just disappeared. His parents didn't know where he was. The police, the FBI and all kinds of private detective agents couldn't find him. Years later, the boy, now a man, finally contacted his parents and told them where he was. He was touring with a carnival in Europe playing the kazoo and enjoying life. He was happy, healthy and thinking about getting married and raising a family.

What is the meaning of this parable?

Needs are often confused by those of us in the human services profession. Counselors, teachers, caseworkers and probation officers often have notions about what is needed for the people they serve. People sometimes have their own interpretation of their own needs and wants. Out of **Dignity and Respect** for each human being, we need to enter into dialogue with him and hopefully clarify which is which.

There is no denying the fact that playing the kazoo in class was a disruptive behavior. How might the playing have been used to support the growth of the boy and still maintain some semblance of order?

When I shared this parable with my wife who teaches first grade, she said, "I'd have the boy play the kazoo every time we were changing subjects. He could be our alarm. He could entertain us while we move from one activity to another one.

His playing would enhance, rather than detract from the learning environment. I might even get a bunch of kazoos and have the whole class learn to play them for music. Why we could even put on a concert for the entire school with the boy conducting and playing the lead solo. Who knows?"
I'm sure that each of you will see many levels of meaning in this story. Read it again and think about what it means for you.

There is no way to treat our people with dignity and respect unless we are with them and meaningfully interacting. We can do this in a casual way or it can be a part of the structure of the program. If we present clear expectations for our people, they are more apt to learn and grow. When we hold people accountable for their behavior and do it in a way that supports their dignity and respect, they are less apt to balk at our intervention in their lives. They will come to appreciate our investment in them. We model dignity and respect by the way we live and by the way we interact with our people. We must treat our team members with dignity and respect, or we won't be able to impact the people we serve. By working together and effectively communicating with one another, we will be more apt to succeed in our efforts to guide people along the path toward healthy, happy and responsible living. We can't realistically hope to implement this principle unless all the other ones are simultaneously being practiced. They are part and parcel to a successful program that provides the highest measure of quality care.

ENVIRONMENT OF CARE

"Maintaining a clean environment that promotes people's physical and mental health"

Environment of Care means we maintain a clean environment that promotes the physical and mental health of the people we serve.

Many times, programs will be concerned about the physical plant, but do not consider how the environment affects the mental health and well being of the people. This may seem strange to say, but from the color of the paint on the walls, to the language we use when addressing people are all part of a continuum that represents the **Environment of Care**.

There isn't anything within any given milieu that can be discounted. I'm sure this seems like a simplistic idea, but let's continue with the thought that we can be sure we fully understand this principle's implications.

I'd like to begin at home. How is your home an **Environment of Care**? What do you do within the four walls to make your family members think and feel their mental and physical health are being cared for day in and out? I'm sure you regularly clean your living space. We clean on Saturday mornings and on Wednesday evenings. Living in the country with dogs, cats and a lot of other factors that require regular cleaning, we've found that twice a week keeps the hair from balling up on the floors and the house from smelling "doggy." Sheets and towels get changed once a week. The nooks and crannies get swabbed once a year. Spring-cleaning has some real meaning in our home because we heat with wood. The soot factor requires that we wipe down the floors and ceilings to get rid of the dinginess left over from the season's heating.

I could elaborate about our own cleaning processes, but I think my point is clear. We clean so that we feel good about the place we live in and are not embarrassed when people come into our home.

Our family esteem and emotional health are taken care of by our hard work and the pride we feel once the home is sparkling again. I can lie down on the couch and look down at the floor and not see dog hair piling up. The clean sheets make me feel good all over. A fresh towel makes me want to take a shower and get out and rub my skin in its soft nap. When I walk onto the porch and see all the sawdust and wood chips are gone and there is only a nice stack of wood ready for the stove, I smile and am thankful that I split the wood in the forest and left most of the mess there. When the place is clean, I'm more apt to want to walk around the house in my bare feet. What a free feeling it is to be wandering around barefoot in the middle of winter. All of these are examples of how a clean environment aids in supporting the mental health of the family.

We are intimately aware of the need to provide a clean environment for the people we serve. An environment in which people can't feel physically well is certainly not one in which care will be of the highest quality. Hospitals probably do this the best because cleanliness is paramount in order to avoid secondary infection. We've all noticed when we've visited a hospital whether or not it is clean. The true measure of a hospital's cleanliness is evident in the visitor's bathrooms and lounges. When these are clean, usually the rest of the hospital is too. We walk away telling ourselves, "This is a nice place." What we mean is that it is a clean, and we are measuring the care it is providing from this one visible factor.

What about the same hospital that has doctors and nurses walking around and treating visitors as if they don't exist? They pass us in the hall, or they come into the room where you are sitting and don't say "Hello," or rudely ask us to leave the room while they "care" for the patient, and then don't bother to thank us for your cooperation. What kind of message does this send? Witnessing actions like this makes us begin to re-evaluate our original premise. The hospital may be physically clean, but the people who work there are rude and unfriendly. We conclude this is one place we wouldn't want to go if we were ill.

The **Environment of Care** has two parts. First, it must be physically clean and safe for all the people we serve to come into it and feel good about being there. So many times, I've been invited to consult with a residential program "in trouble" meaning that the staff aren't doing what they're supposed to do and they know it. My fresh eyes and ears are invited in to provide some guidance and support. When they invite my eyes and ears, they also invite my nose, my hands and my taste buds.

The first two places I go to make my assessment of the program are the bathroom and the cafeteria. I walk into the men's room and look around, smell the air, touch the sink and feel if it is clean or not. I notice if the baskets are emptied and the urinals and toilet stalls are clean. I check to see if there is toilet paper in the dispenser and soap on the sink. When the bathroom is unkempt, I begin to wonder how the rest of the program is creating an "environment of care?" Now, a clean bathroom can sometimes fake me out so I look more closely at my next stop.

My next stop is the cafeteria. Here it is much more difficult to hide things. This is a veritable smorgasbord of information. How appealing is the food being served? How is it being served? Are the food service employees polite to the patrons? Am I able to get what I want or do they just slop some gruel down on my plate and pass it to me? How comfortable are the chairs? Are the people who live there polite? Do the words "please" and "thank you" flow through conversations? How are the employees who are eating with the clients interacting with them? Is there a sense of urgency to eat and run, or are people sitting still and enjoying their meals while talking with one another in a way that models meaningful interaction?

I could continue but you get the point. An **Environment of Care** should really be a pleasant place. It smells, sounds, tastes, feels and looks inviting. If it doesn't, then, my readers, it is not. We can't pretend we have an **Environment of Care** when these simple tests show we don't. An environment of care promotes the physical and mental health of the people it serves. When it does not, we are going to be struggling to implement all the other principles. In fact, if the environment doesn't support our mission and philosophy, we will inevitably fail and sometimes miserably. How can we say we care about our people when the environment communicates a different message?

This simple litmus test for evaluating a program works almost as well as the scientific one. I recall visiting a struggling program and taught the principles. I was invited to return months later to see how well things were going.

When I walked into the same program, the environment was clean, the food service was pleasant and the sights, sounds, smells, touch and taste of the place were vastly improved. I found the quality of care in other areas improved as well. Groups occurred on time. Transition from one place to another was done in an orderly fashion. The people treated one another with dignity and respect. Though I was a stranger, people walked up to me and made me feel welcome. They introduced themselves to me. They thanked me for coming to visit. They invited me in for a cup of coffee. They showed me where the restrooms were. They asked me if I'd like to take a tour of the program. Now, I like that offer because it gives me more time to continue my assessment. In general, I found the place vastly improved and it is a joy to put in my report to the directors who initially invited me that everything was vastly improved.

It's such a neat feeling to see an **Environment of Care** develop. The change is a spiritually moving experience for me because I can believe that the people being served are receiving a higher quality of care. True, other factors need to be taken into consideration, but this initial change is the place to start. The physical plant becomes a model for the clients receiving treatment and for those who work there. When things are busy, it's not an easy task to keep the physical plant clean. Yet, think about it. It's the easiest thing to fix right away.

Cleaning an environment is the place to start. First, the physical environment gets more than a lick and a polish. The nooks and crannies are scrubbed clean. A white glove test is used to make sure that the job is done with integrity.

Once the team gets the physical plant in tip-top shape, then it's on to the mental cleanliness. The quality of the human interactions is addressed. Profanity and vulgarity disappear, and the highest level of human interaction is taking place. People refer to each other by their first or last names, not nicknames or slang terms. Have you ever been in a program where the people being served were referred to as "loonies" or "little darlings" or "the crips" or "tards" or a host of truly disrespectful names? What does this tell you about the mental health concerns? You can believe that the team responsible isn't doing its best to care for them. Their language is derogatory. If they use disrespectful language with an outsider like me, just imagine what the people in the program get to hear on a daily basis?

I work with youth. In general, I call them "Gentlemen" and "Ladies". I don't call them boys and girls. I want them to act like young men and women so I refer to them as such. But there is an affectionate name I use and that is "kids" because at heart that's what they still are. I've not found the youth to be offended by this affectionate term. I've seen their reaction though when I've heard them referred to as "boys and girls." If they react to it, I don't use it. It sounds disrespectful and detracts from the **Environment of Care**. If it seems like I'm overlapping into **Dignity and Respect**, you're right. It's pretty hard not to do so. These principles are Siamese twins. It's rare to find one being practiced without the other and vice versa. When one is out of kilter, so is the other.

There is nothing more exciting to see a program change the **Environment of Care** with the team members and the youth working side by side improving the whole place.

This is truly one of the most impressive metamorphoses a program can undertake. I've been privileged to watch it happen over and over again. I've been doubly blessed when it's been the result of simple feedback I've shared with the team. I fully believe that once the environment or care is improved, everything else falls into place in a relatively short period of time.

Please don't misunderstand me. I'm not saying that there needs to be a rage for order to keep a place clean and neat. Sometimes we go overboard in trying to achieve this principle. For instance, if you work in a residential setting, you know how important it is for the people who live there to feel at home. Yes, it must be clean, but at the same times, rooms need to be a reflection of the people who live in them. Dirty underwear do not belong in the middle of a bedroom floor. Toothbrushes need to be put away, not lying carelessly on the edge of a desk. Lockers need to be neat and orderly and the doors closed. But what about pictures on the walls or bulletin boards and books stacked on a desk? What about the poster that a person hangs on the wall that may inspire him to be happier and healthier? It is important to consider within a program's environment, the personal expression of the people who live there. If we become so rigid about how it should look and sound and smell, we may lose the essence of what the principle truly means. Many times I've visited programs where the rooms were all alike. The walls were painted a standard oyster shell white. The lobbies, offices and other work and living spaces seemed to me so sterile I wanted to get up and leave. Color adds something to an environment. Individual expression in work places and living quarters adds the important dimension that any program can foster and that is self-expression. Let me illustrate this by telling a story.

Parable of the Locker

A few years ago, I was asked to facilitate a change process in a residential program. What I remember the most was how really awful the environment was. It was the first place we focused our change efforts. One client, whom I met during the initial days of the project, cussed me out for coming into his "home" and feeding the team a bunch of "bull." I smiled and went on my way, but not without thinking about this young man.

How could I implement a change process and fail to engage him in it? I struggled with this for a month. We cleaned. We intervened in youth's lives. We taught people how to do group facilitation and then restructured every aspect of the program. We wrote a new clinical program and implemented it.

A month after I arrived, I was walking around on a Sunday morning and I heard someone call my name. It was the client who had given me a full load of disrespect. He asked me to come into his room. I said sure and entered wondering what he wanted to share with me. "Look at my locker," he directed me.

I opened the door and looked inside. It was impeccable. Socks and shirts were neatly folded. Shirts were ironed and hanging up to keep them from being wrinkled. His shoes were lined up on the floor. His dirty clothes were safely stored in a mesh bag hanging on the side of the locker. His towels were drying on hangers.

I was impressed and told him so. "I'll bet you never thought I'd get it together?" he blurted out. I smiled and said, "No, quite frankly, I just wondered how long it would take for you to accept responsibility for your own life. That's all."

He smiled at me and said, "I'm sorry for cussing you out when we first met. I thought you were here just to make trouble. I could tell you were firing up the staff and they were going to make our lives miserable. Fact is things are better, I feel better and so I'm sorry." Before I left, he showed me some drawings he made in school. They were hanging neatly on his bulletin board.

He reached to shake my hand. I asked him for a hug instead. We parted company and I went on my way with a much lighter step. The seeds were beginning to produce fruit.

A month earlier, this young man wanted to knock my head off. Now we had made peace. What made the difference? Once he started to live in an **Environment of Care**, I truly believe he started to care about himself. It took a month for him to get the message, but he got it. This is all that mattered. My role as change agent got easier and easier as the team worked with the clients and made the entire environment one in which the physical and mental health of all the clients was maintained on a daily basis.

Have you ever been in a fine nursing home where the elderly get quality care? What is it that first catches your attention? Yes, it's the smell. The place doesn't reek of urine and feces. It smells clean. Aides are moving around all over the place insuring that the people who live there are clean and comfortable.

Many elderly suffer from incontinence. In this milieu, it is essential for the team to care for them. If they do this with this principle in mind, they are more apt to provide an **Environment of Care** that is truly healthy.

It's more than just cleaning the place to meet licensing requirements. It's more than trying to make a good impression on the visitors who come and go but don't live there. It means they provide this extraordinary **Environment of Care** because it is one of their principles.

It symbolizes "Best Practice." They do it because they believe in their mission and our principles. These are the alpha and omega of providing quality care.

Hospitals often err on the side of anesthetic approach to an **Environment of Care.** They are clean but people don't feel good about being there. Some of this is only natural. Who wants to be in a hospital? It usually means one thing. We're not okay in some way. It is essential for hospital personnel to work hard to create a place that is mentally healthy. The movie, *Patch Adams*, illustrates this principle to the utmost. If you haven't seen it and you work in the hospital setting, please get it and spend time really listening to the message and watching how it is delivered. I don't believe that only hospital health care teams would benefit though by watching the movie. We all can because the message is about an **Environment of Care**. Adams believed that the environment was as important as the medical care being given. He went out of his way to insure that the people lying in the beds were as happy as they could be. He did whatever it took to make them happy.

What about those of you who work in the human service profession in outpatient counseling centers, day treatment programs, or provide services to teens at risk through probation departments or "Big Brothers" or "Big Sisters" Clubs? How does this principle apply to you since you don't have people staying with you in your place of work? Let me respond to your inquiry in this way.

You don't have people with you twenty-four-seven like residential or health care centers do, but you do have youth coming into your milieu for a period of time every day? What impression do they get when they come into your agency, office, cafeteria, bathrooms or parking lot? How are they greeted? What do they experience when they are asked to wait in a lobby? What kind of atmosphere is present? What non-verbal messages are communicated? They only pass through your lives in short bursts of time. It becomes even more important for you to insure that everything about your environment promotes quality care. As the commercial says, "You don't get a second chance to make a first impression." If the **Environment of Care** in your agency needs work, you can change it. The change itself will communicate to the people you serve that you are committed to quality care. What else can there be to say about it? You either commit to doing it or it doesn't get done.

A program facelift doesn't cost a lot of money. It may require some elbow grease, warm soap and water and a willingness to get things sparkling again. It might require team meetings to assess the current state of the mental health aspects of the program and design strategies to improve them. Then it requires we implement them and watch the results. It may demand that we ask for feedback from those we serve and get their insight. If we do this with an open mind and heart, they will tell us the truth. It's especially rewarding when a program takes on a major change and then gets feedback from the clients who really appreciate the hard work done to make them feel welcome, comfortable and appreciated. At moments like these, it makes all the hard work worthwhile. It makes all of us beam with joy, with pride, and want to keep it this way.

The principle of **Environment of Care** doesn't have any meaning or doesn't really matter where people don't care.

We cannot implement this principle without simultaneously doing all the other principles of quality care. They are linked together like septuplets. They come from the same parents. They are brothers and sisters to one another. They are all unique and separate from one another. Like a family, they are bonded together.

We meaningfully interact with our people so that we can insure that they learn to be responsible, happy, healthy human beings. We do this in a program that exhibits a high degree of structure and provides clear expectations for the change that we plan will take place. We teach responsibility by expecting people to accept accountability for their behavior. We affirm them when they do, and we address their behavior when they are not. We teach them most effectively when we model the behaviors, attitudes and beliefs we want them to learn. We engage them in working with us to make a difference in their lives. We know they alone can do it, but they can't do it alone. Neither can we do it for them. Working as a team, anything is possible. With dignity and respect for all those we serve, we approach each and every person we are responsible for with the highest quality of care we can provide because they are just like us - human beings with needs. Lastly, when we function in an environment that promotes the physical and mental health of those we serve, we insure that they will receive quality care.

Doing anything less than all of this would be unprofessional.

PUTTING PRINCIPLES INTO PRACTICE

How do we put it all together? After all, this is the essence of learning anything. We want to use what we have learned to better the lives of those we serve. Otherwise, what is the purpose in learning something?

With this thought in mind, let me tell another parable.

Parable of the Reluctant Sleeper

A client named Doug was refusing to go to bed. He was supposed to be sleeping in the hallway because he threatened his roommate. His mattress was on the floor outside his room. The clinical team placed him on intense supervision to isolate him until he could meet with his primary counselor in the morning. He was leaning up against the wall when the supervisor walked into the unit.

"What's Doug doing up?" the supervisor asked.

"He's refusing to go to bed."

"Well, tell him to go to bed."

"He's refusing. Could you help us out?" the clinician asked.

"What do you want to do?"

"Get him into bed."

"So tell him to go to bed."

"We did but he's refusing to go."

"If I tell him to go to bed and he does, I'll be undermining your position."

"We still think we need some help here."

"How can I help?"

"We just can't seem to get him to cooperate. Can you show us how to do it?"

"I can, but let's do this as a team. He needs to get one message from all of us."

"Okay. We got it."

Another clinician comes over and they begin to intervene with Doug.

"Doug, it's time to go to bed. Please get up from the floor and get into your bed."

"I don't want to go to bed. Leave me alone," Doug blurts out.

"It's time to go to bed. Please get up now and get into your bed. The expectation is that you go to bed when you're told."

"I don't want to go to bed and you can't make me."

"No, we can't make you. The expectation is that you go to bed now. You will learn to be responsible here. You have some choices. Right now we'd like *you to consider doing what is in your best interest," Clinician two says.*

Doug stops to think. "Leave me alone."

"We're going to leave you alone as soon as you get into bed. Right now, we're going to make sure everyone else is in bed. Then we'll be back. You think about what's in your best interest."

The team leaves Doug sitting up against the wall. One clinician stays with him and continues to talk to him. Doug still refuses. The team discusses what to do next.

The two clinicians ask the supervisor why he didn't make Doug get into bed. The supervisor responds by telling them that Doug will make a choice and then we'll respond to it. The clinicians are frustrated.

The supervisor tells them that the real growth for Doug will come when he makes a choice. His refusal is his way of continuing to remain in control. The choice to remain in control is going to produce consequences that Doug may not like.

By the time they get back to Doug, he has left the hallway. He's gone back into the room where his roommate, the client he threatened, is trying to sleep. The supervisor and the clinicians discuss what may happen when they go in to get Doug. He tells the team that if Doug won't leave the room willingly, they will escort him to the hallway and his bed.

"Doug may react. If he does, then we will need to respond. Hopefully, he will do what's in his best interest. We'll use the hook and carry if we need to move him." Are we all are in agreement?"

They go into the room where Doug is in bed.

"Doug, we notice you're back in your bed, but the mattress for your bed is in the hallway for a reason. That is where you're supposed to be sleeping. You're being isolated because of the threats you made tonight."

"I'm not moving. I'm in bed. I'm doing what you told me to do."

"You were asked to think about doing what's in your best interest. Right now, *you are doing just what you want to do without considering the consequences.*
What are you going to do?"

Doug sits in silence.

"Doug, we're asking you a question."

Doug doesn't respond. He is silent.

The team waits for five minutes for Doug to make a decision.

"Doug, please get up and go to your bed."

"Make me."

"We are simply asking you to go to your bed and lie down. We are asking you to be responsible. We're not asking you to do anything that is illegal, immoral, unhealthy or unethical. We're asking you to be a responsible person."

Doug is again silent.

"Doug, what are you going to do right now that is in your best interest?"

"I'm not going to do what you tell me."

"We've asked you a number of times to be cooperative. You have consistently refused to cooperate. Now I'm telling you to get up and move to your bed and go to sleep."

"Make me," says Doug in a challenging tone of voice.

"We don't want to make you. We want you to demonstrate self-control and get *up and go to bed. That's all. Nothing complicated.*"

"I'm not moving. You're going to have to move me."

"We can do that, but we'd prefer that you move yourself."

"Do it then."

Team gets in position. The supervisor and clinicians carefully lift Doug up from the bed using a hook and carry team procedure for moving a client safely from one place to another.

"Leave me alone," Doug hollers.

"Doug, we're not going to hurt you. All we want you to do is get in bed."

"Leave me alone," Doug screams starting to struggle.

"Please cooperate with us and we won't have to move you."

Doug locks his legs into the bed and resists the move. The supervisor and clinicians slowly ease Doug off the bed. As they move him, Doug snaps his head back and hits the supervisor with his head.

"Please don't do that, Doug. That hurts."

"Leave me alone or I'll do it again."

"I'd prefer that you don't."

"Then leave me alone."

The supervisor and the clinicians escort Doug out of his room using the hook and carry. Doug struggles and tries to hit the supervisor again. He is told to get in control. He continues to be aggressive.

"Doug, stop being aggressive. Please get control of yourself."

Doug continues to head butt the supervisor. The supervisor takes control by using an upper torso assist to restrict Doug's aggressive moves."Leave me alone. I'm going to get you."

"Doug, we're not trying to hurt you. We asked you a number of times to go to bed. You refused. We directed you to go. You refused. We carefully assisted *you to move and now you've started to be aggressive. Please get back in control."*

Doug continues to head butt the supervisor. He uses an Upper Torso Assist to the floor to gain more control. The team quickly assists and places Doug in a multiple person floor position with one clinician restricting Doug's left arm.

The supervisor restricts Doug's right arm movement. The other clinician bridges the legs. They tell Doug that he is safe, that he is not going to be hurt, and that he needs to get back into control. They tell him that when he's ready to make commitments, they will listen.

Doug is verbally abusive for about a half-hour. The team doesn't respond to his threats and abuse. They just tell him to get back in control. After 40 minutes of this,

Doug calms down. He is silent for a long period of time. Nearly an hour passes before Doug is willing to make commitments. The team continues to use therapeutic holds with Doug until he finally decides to make commitments. As he does, the team slowly releases his arms and legs. When he is sitting on the floor, the team checks Doug for any possible injuries, bruises or abrasions. Doug says he doesn't hurt anywhere. The team then asks Doug if he is ready to do the Life Space Interview, the therapeutic process that helps the client to integrate new learning.

"Doug, in order to learn something from this incident, we need to process this experience with you. We'd like to do the life space interview with you right now. Will you make a commitment to do this with us?"

"Yes, I will. I hear you."

"Okay, let's begin. Doug, what was your perception of what took place in his *incident?*"

Doug thinks about it for a moment. "I was told to go to bed and I refused to go. Then I went into my room and I knew I wasn't supposed to go there because I threatened my roommate and was supposed to sleep in the hallway until tomorrow when I would talk to my counselor."

"What else?"

"No. That's about it," Doug says.

"Thanks for sharing that with us and for cooperating right now. So let us share with you what our perceptions are of the incident that took place a little while ago. We asked you to go to bed. You repeatedly refused. Then you went into your room where you were told not to go. When we came in to ask you to move back out into the hallway, you again refused. We asked you a number of times to move but you continued to refuse. We then directed you to move and you still refused. Then, we carefully assisted you to move by lifting you up from the bed. At that time, you became aggressive, using your head to butt the supervisor. He asked you to stop, but you tried again and again to hit him. He finally took you safely to the floor and then we all engaged and physically held you while you continued to struggle. Eventually you calmed down and made commitments to cooperate and now we're here sitting in peace, talking."

"That's about it," Doug replies.

"Doug, how is the incident that took place a little while ago a pattern of behavior that you've seen developing in your lifetime?"

Doug thinks for a moment. "That's pretty easy to answer. Whenever I get told to do something, I get the urge to resist. It's like the devil takes hold of me and I can't stop myself from doing what I did. I can almost feel the evil taking over. It's like I have no control over it even though I know it really was in my best interest to just go to bed. My father used to have a hard time getting me to go to bed. I'd just refuse. He'd try and make me but I'd punch him. He's smaller than me so he has to be careful. I might hurt him. I know that I was wrong. I just can't help myself sometimes. I didn't hurt you did I? I'm really sorry for butting you. Are you okay? I'm really sorry about that. You sure you're okay?"

"I'm alright. Thanks for asking. It would have been better had you listened to what we were saying. You might have avoided a lot of grief."

"Tell me about it. I know that I was way out of line."

"What things could you have done differently in this situation that would have produced different results?"

Doug thinks for a moment.

"I could have just done what I was told. I could have just gone to bed. If I hadn't made the threats earlier in the day, I'd have been sleeping in my own bed and not in the hallway being watched so that I didn't try and hurt my roommate. I could have stopped when I was on the floor in the hallway and just crawled into bed. I could have just kept my mouth shut and my ears open. There are a lot of things I could've done differently. I could take the devil in me and not let him get control. I don't like it when I lose control. It takes me feel like a little kid and I'm not a kid any more. I've got to grow up some day. It's embarrassing to be held down on the floor and not be able to move. I'm sorry for those nasty things I said to you both."

"You can be nasty when you're out of control. It's much more pleasant sitting here like this just talking. You know we weren't going to hurt you. But when you started trying to hurt others, we need to make sure that everyone is safe, including you and the rest of your peers."

"I know. I know. I've got to get it together.

"Now, are you ready for bed?"

"Yes, I am, but could I go to the bathroom and brush my teeth first?"

"Sure, let's go. I have to use the restroom too."

"Sorry again about hitting you. I just was out of control."

"I know that, but right now, you've got four or five other things you could have done, and we'll expect you to use them the next time you get frustrated and the Devil gets a hold of you."

Doug laughs. "I can't believe you're not upset with me."

"I'm not upset with you because I knew eventually you would get back in control and realize just how irresponsible you were being. Now that you're back in control, you have the chance to learn something of real value and not have to repeat this situation ever again. If you so choose, of course."

"I hear you."

"Tomorrow will be a better day."

"I'm really tired now," Doug says.

"So am I," the supervisor says.

"Can I go to the bathroom and brush my teeth and go to bed?"

"Go to the bathroom, Doug."

"Yes sir." Doug gets up to leave.

"Before you go, though, let me show you a neat move. It's called the reverse upper torso," the supervisor says.

Doug looks confused. "I'm in control now. I've had enough for one night."

"I know you're in control, but let me show you the move."

The supervisor hugs Doug.

Doug laughs. "I like that move better. It's not as rough."

"Goodnight. Now go to bed."

"I'm off to bed..."

One of the clinicians asks, "You covering the incident report and the life space interview case note?"

The supervisor says, "Got it. You take care of Doug and by the time you get back I'll have the paperwork finished and you can review it."

"Will do."

Doug and the clinician go to the bathroom. The supervisor goes to the office and completes the paperwork. Once Doug is in bed, the supervisor and the clinician sit down and process the incident and decide what they could have done better. The clinician reviews the paperwork and makes a comment or two. The supervisor makes the necessary revisions and then writes the particulars about the incident in the team communication log. The supervisor makes one last stop at Doug's bed.

"You okay Doug. No aches or pains anywhere?"

"No sir."

"The nurse will check you out in the morning just to make sure that you don't have any injuries that show up over night."

"I'm okay. But thanks for asking again."

"We just want to make sure, that's all."

"How's your head."

"Harder than yours."

They both laugh.

"Good night, Doug. Say your prayers."

"I will. I need to pray for self-control."

"A little divine intervention never hurts. Good night, Doug."

"Good night. See you tomorrow."

"Yes you will and tomorrow will be a better day. A brand new day. Another drug and alcohol free day."

"Amen to that," Doug says.

"I'm out of here."

"Have a safe trip home."

"Amen to that too."

The lights go out.

Many of you may never face a situation like this one. There is no crisis that evokes such strong emotional responses in human service workers as a passive aggressive person who will not cooperate, and then, when he's had enough of his own passivity, becomes aggressive. The initial gut reaction in most of us is to either take flight or to fight. Reflecting back to Chapter 3, recall that we need to overcome this natural human response and use this opportunity to teach the person some new coping skills. We need to challenge his thinking so that he can be more in control the next time he is faced with a situation that causes him to want to explode. We must accept responsibility to take every opportunity and teach our people to be in control.

Given all the types of behaviors that we deal with in our profession, passive aggression that leads to outright physical assault, evokes the most amount of conflict in us. Doug was being passive aggressive.

How do we get him to do what is responsible? In this situation, he was placed on intense supervision to monitor his behavior so that he wouldn't continue to threaten anyone else. Using his scene, let's assess what principles were being applied to effectively intervene with Doug?

First, the team was with Doug and meaningfully interacting with him. Getting a person to go to bed may not appear to be a glamorous clinical activity, but it is necessary for the person to learn that there are boundaries in life.

At no time was Doug left alone. He was being monitored for his own safety and that of the other clients.

Second, the team gave him clear expectations. Bedtime was 10 o'clock. Over and over again, they asked, then told him to go to bed. Doug was violating the norm. They made it clear to him that he needed to get into bed. They even waited in silence for him to make a decision. Finally, they assisted him by staying with him until he successfully followed the expectation.

Third, they were trying to teach him to be responsible for himself by expecting him to accept accountability for his behavior. He didn't want to do it. He wanted to resist. They considered the *Principles of Resistance* and tried to patiently wait him out. There is a limit to the amount of time we can wait though, and sometimes, as in this case, we may need to assist the person to do what we are asking. As the team member said, "We're not asking you to do anything illegal, immoral, unhealthy, or unethical. We are merely asking you to get in bed."

The lessons we often teach are simple ones, but they have far reaching implications. When Doug can begin to follow a simple direction like "Go to bed", then he will have developed the skills and self-control necessary to follow more complex ones.

The team was engaging him in dialogue only to the extent that he was moving toward the expected outcome. It isn't a magical process. The team asked him to do what was in his best interest, but he refused.

At times, people will do that, but in general, they will do what is in their best interest. As Freud hypothesized, human beings seek pleasure and avoid pain.

Some of our people don't function normally and sometimes, they accept life's pain as normal and tolerable. When they begin to really change, they start to make decisions that support Freud's theory.

Fourth, the team members were being positive role models for Doug. They didn't react to his refusal. They continued to use logic, reason, compassion, and persistence to get him to do what he was supposed to do. They didn't raise their voices and holler at him even though he was being difficult. I must admit that I didn't include in the parable, any of the foul language Doug used. This was because I didn't want to offend your eyes. Doug was verbally abusive as well as physically aggressive. During the period of time the team was on the floor with Doug, they were quiet, didn't talk to him or to each other very much. They were modeling patience for him. Eventually, the fatigue and the silence wore him out.

Fifth, teamwork and communication were present from the beginning to the end. The supervisor was asked to assist because the team was not making progress. He said, "I don't want to undermine your authority. Let's do this together with one voice." He was aware of the need to present a unified team position so that Doug could not use triangulation - work one team member against another. The team talked about what they were going to do, planned for the possibility of an explosion, and when it occurred, handled it safely.

Sixth, they treated Doug with dignity and respect. He needed to go to bed. This was the expectation, the direction, the program norm and the team clearly communicated this to him. They didn't holler at him, and they gave him every opportunity to get into bed by himself. They asked him a number of times to go. They waited for a full five minutes in silence to give him the opportunity to comply with the request. They directed him to go and waited again.

Finally, carefully, they were attempting to assist him to get into bed and he made a choice to explode. Once he became aggressive, they abandoned the non-verbal and verbal intervention strategies and physically intervened. They safely continued with a physical intervention using therapeutic holds to safely secure Doug while he continued his aggression. They continued until Doug was no longer a danger to himself or others. Once he was ready to make commitments, they began the release process. After Doug was released, they spent another significant period of time processing the incident doing the life space interview. This was the therapeutic part of the intervention. By asking Doug the questions they did, they were guiding him in integrating new learning. Doug was open to their inquiry and learned a number of new ways in which he could behave differently the next time he was faced with this type of situation.

Seventh, the team provided an environment of care. They were careful to protect Doug's physical well being and they worked hard to insure that his mental state of being was protected too. They didn't insult him, blame him for his behavior or chastise him for being difficult. They were trying to teach him how to manage his own life.
I believe you will agree that they accomplished what they set out to do.

How do we know that we're effectively applying **the Principles of Quality Care**? We must know what they are. It's essential that we know them by heart. We can't use them if we don't know them. We need to be able to define the principle and understand and be able to apply all concepts that are a part of the principle. Each one contains a number of concepts. **People Security** contains "being with people" AND "meaningfully interacting with them." In order to be effective in applying this one, we must be able to do both parts. This is true for all the rest of the principles.

What are the principles again?

7 Key Principles

People Security: Being with people and meaningfully interacting with them

Program Integrity: Providing a high degree of structure and clear expectations for change

ARE: Teaching responsibility by expecting people to accept accountability for their behavior

Positive Role Modeling: Teaching people by setting an example

Teamwork & Communication: Working together and effectively communicating with one another

Dignity and Respect: Showing care and concern for all peoples' needs

Environment of Care: Maintaining a clean environment that promotes peoples' physical and mental health

By understanding the principles in concept form, it is easier to learn them. We can easily get overwhelmed if we try and learn them all at one time, or apply them without having some strategy to integrate them into our programs. It is essential to learn each one separately, learn the definition and then use it. Once we're absolutely clear what makes it important as a principle that supports quality care we can then find ways to apply it in our programs on a daily basis.

There is a special joy that emanates from principle-centered living. The mystery of our work disappears. We fully comprehend the awesome nature of the work we do. We serve people. We do so through the use of principles that focus our energies and result in our being able to provide quality care. The well being of any human is too important to leave our interventions to chance. In order to be successful in our mission, we must be grounded on sound principles in which we can believe in, principles that work, principles that are simple to implement and engage human beings in the change process.

To this end, I believe you have before you such a set of principles.

As the band Pink Floyd says at the end of Dark Side of the Moon, "There's nothing more to say."

Thanks for taking the time to read this book.

"Now, go and do good work."

REFERENCES

Adler, Mortimer J. THE DIFFERENCE IN MAN AND THE DIFFERENCE IT MAKES. New York: Allayed, Rinehart and Winston, 1967.

Bandura, A. "Behavior Theory and the Models of Man," AMERICAN PSYCHIATRIST, 1974, 29, 859-69.

Bandura, A. (1969). Principles of behavior modification. New York: Holt, Rinehart and Winston, Inc.

Bandura, A., & Walters, R.H. (1963). Social learning and personality development. New York: Holt, Rinehart, and Winston, Inc.

Bandura, A., & Walters, R.H. (1963). Adolescent aggression. New York: The Ronald Press Co.

Braukman, C.J., et al. (1975). Behavioral approaches to treatment in the crime and delinquency field. Criminology, 13,3, 300-319.

BIBLE, The New Revised Standard Edition

Bufford, Rodger K. THE HUMAN REFLEX. New York: Harper and Row, 1981.

Carpenter, F. THE SKINNER PRIMER. New York: The Free Press, 1974.

Chomsky, N. "Review of Verbal Behavior", LANGUAGE, 1959, 35, 26-58.

Clark, Gordon H. BEHAVIORISM AND CHRISTIANITY. Jefferson, MD.: The Trinity Foundation, 1982.

Cosgrove, Mark. B.F. SKINNER'S BEHAVIORISM: AN ANALYSIS. Grand Rapids, MI.: Zondervan, 1982.

Cosgrove, Mark. THE ESSENCE OF HUMAN NATURE. Grand Rapids, MI.: Zondervan, 1977.

Custance, Arthur C. THE MYSTERIOUS MIND OF MAN. Grand Rapids, MI.: Zondervan, 1980.

Evans, Stephen C. PRESERVING THE PERSON. Downers Grove, IL.: Inter-varsity Press, 1977.

Eysenck, H.J. (1978). Crime and personality. London: Routledge and Kegan Paul.

Gendreau, P., & Ross, B. (1979). Effective correctional treatment: Bibliotherapy for cynics. Crime and Delinquency, 25,4, 21-33.

Hilts, Philip J. BEHAVIOR MODIFICATION. New York: Harpers Magazine Press, 1974.

Kohlberg, L. (1958). The development of modes of moral thinking and choice in years 10 to 16. Unpublished Doctoral dissertation. University of Chicago.

Kohlberg, L. (1963). The development of children's' orientations toward moral order. Vita Humana, 6,2, 11-13.

Kohlberg, L. (1968). The child as moral philosopher. Psychology Today, 2,31, 24-31.

Kohlberg, L. (1980). Moral development, moral education, and Kohlberg. In Brendan Munsey, ed., The Philosophy of Moral Development.

Kohlberg, L., & Tapp, J.L. (1971). Developing senses of law and legal justice. Journal of Social Issues, 27,23, 75.

Kohlberg, L., & Tapp, J.L. (1970). A child's garden of law and order. Psychology Today, 4, 29-31.

Lewis. C.S. THE ABOLITION OF MAN. New York: MacMillan, 1947.

Machan, Tibor R. THE PSEUDO-SCIENCE OF B.F. SKINNER. New Rochelle, NY.: Arlington House, 1974.

Matson, Floyd W. THE BROKEN IMAGE. New York: Doubleday, 1964.

Matson, Floyd W. THE IDEA OF MAN. New York: Delacorte, 1976.

Morash, M.A. (1981). Cognitive developmental theory: A basis for juvenile correctional reform. Criminology, 19,3, 360-371.

Nemcik, Bert. (1999). I Think, Therefore: I'm Free. Unpublished manuscript. Lifelong Learning Network, 1999.

Popper, Karl R. and Eccles, John C. THE SELF AND ITS BRAIN. Berlin: Springer-Verlag, 1977.

Rogers, Carl and Skinner, B.F. "Some issues concerning the control of human behavior," SCIENCE. 1956. 124, 1057-1066.

Sagi, A., & Eisikovits, Z. (1981). Juvenile delinquency and moral development. Criminal Justice and Behavior, 8,1, 79-93.

Samenow, S.E. (1984). Inside the criminal mind. New York: Times Books.

Samenow, S.E. (1989). Before it's too late. New York: Times Books.

Samenow, S.E., & Yochelson, S. (1976). The criminal personality. Scranton, PA: Jason Arons. Vol. 1: Profile for Change. Vol. 2: The Change Process. Vol. 3: The Drug User.

Schaeffer, Francis A. BACK TO FREEDOM AND DIGNITY. Downers Grove, IL.: Inter-varsity Press, 1972.

Skinner, B.F. ABOUT BEHAVIORISM. New York: Alfred A. Knopf, 1974.

Skinner, B.F. BEYOND AND FREEDOM AND DIGNITY. New York: Alfred A. Knopf, 1971.

Skinner, B.F. (1953). Science and human behavior. New York: Macmillan.

Skinner, B.F. (1974). About behaviorism. New York: Alfred A. Knopf.

Skinner, B.F. (1978). Reflections on behaviorism and society. Englewood Cliffs, NJ: Prentice-Hall.

TIME. Sept. 20, 1971. "Skinner's Utopia: Panacea, or Path to Hell."

AUTHOR'S BIO

From 1991 until 2011, Bert Nemcik, Ph.D., served as the Training Director for the Cornell Training Institute. He started working with difficult youth in 1969 with the Ohio Youth Commission. He taught junior high school in Youngstown, Ohio.

In 1972, he went to work with his father at US Steel in Youngstown, Ohio. He spent six years working in a steel mill with his father. He accepted a position with Cornell Abraxas in 1979.

During his tenure with Cornell Abraxas, he taught English and Math, Industrial Arts, was a senior counselor, family counselor, founder of the Abraxas Wilderness Experience and a wilderness leader, assistant clinical director, senior treatment supervisor and coordinator of court reporting.

In 1993, Bert founded the Lifelong Learning Network, an internet-education, training and consulting firm. He's written more than 15 books and dozens of training manuals on subjects like cultural differences, intensive treatment programming, effective interventions, the therapeutic use of passive restraint, behavior modification, boundary issues, ethics education and how to train trainers.

Bert has been the lead trainer in eleven new program initiatives in the past ten years.

Bert is an avid cyclist and commutes to work nine months a year on his mountain bike. In 1995, he rode solo across America from Oregon to New Jersey 3165 miles on his bicycle raising more than $20,000 for Habitat for Humanity, his favorite charity.

In 2002, he thru-hiked the Appalachian Trail from Maine to Georgia, a journey of 2170 miles.

For the past twenty-two years, he's written a weekly column for the Forest Press entitled, "Life, Liberty and Library".

Cheryl, Bert's wife, is a retired first grade teacher.

His son, Ethan, finished a four-year tour of duty with the US ARMY in Germany, and now lives in Greeley, Colorado. Bert's motto is: "You don't have a problem IF you have a solution."

In 2011, Bert retired from his professional career and now spends winters writing fiction and non-fiction books, and spring, summer and autumn hiking, backpacking, fishing, camping, kayaking, mountain climbing, hunting medicinal herbs, motorcycling and working on his small ranch in south central Colorado.

Bert can be contacted at bnemcik@yahoo.com.